The Re-Discovery
of
Common Sense!

The Re-Discovery
of
Common Sense!

A Guide to:
The Lost Art of Critical Thinking

Chuck Clayton

iUniverse, Inc.
New York Lincoln Shanghai

The Re-Discovery of Common Sense
A Guide to the Lost Art of Critical Thinking

iUniverse books may be ordered through booksellers or by contacting:

iUniverse
2021 Pine Lake Road, Suite 100
Lincoln, NE 68512
www.iuniverse.com
1-800-Authors (1-800-288-4677)

Because of the dynamic nature of the Internet, any Web addresses or links contained in this book may have changed since publication and may no longer be valid.

ISBN: 978-0-595-43708-5 (pbk)
ISBN: 978-0-595-88040-9 (ebk)

Printed in the United States of America

Dedication

This book is dedicated to **Fallon Gates** and to **Blade Gates** for they are part of the next generation of critical thinkers!

Contents

Acknowledgments... xiii

Introduction xv
  Our Most Powerful Strength............................ xv
  What are Critical Thinking Skills? xvi
  Why You Need Critical Thinking Skills xviii
  America's Universities xviii
  Where Do We Go From Here?..........................xix

The Foundation 1

Chapter 1   Key Elements of Critical Thinking 3
  A Curious and Open Mind...............................3
  Thinking through Issues 4
  Analyze Issues from Multiple View Points 6
  Doing Needed Investigation 8
  Intuitive and Non-Intuitive Thinking.....................8
  Can Your Critical Thinking Skills be Improved? 12
  Looking Forward...13

Chaptet 2   Land Mines to Critical Thinking!...............14
  Egocentric Thinking 15
  Social Conditioning......................................16
  Biased Experience 16

Arrogance and Intolerance 17

Time and Patience. 17

Group Think—The Herd Mentality. 18

The Drone Mentality 19

Sidestepping the Land Mines 20

Looking Forward. 21

Chapter 3   What are some Critical Questions? 22

Information and Information Sources. 23

Assumptions 24

Interpretations and Implications 25

Conclusions. 25

Looking Forward. 26

Critical Thinking Methods and Resources 27

Chapter 4   How to Solve Mysteries! 29

Experts who have solved the Mystery of Their Field 29

How to Solve Mysteries using Critical Thinking 31

The Scientific Method. 32

The 80/20 Rule 34

Tinkering, the Art of Playing 36

Locating the Root Cause of Problems. 38

Working Backwards. 42

Using History as a Guide. 43

Looking Forward. 44

Chapter 5   How to Investigate any Subject 45

Just in Time Learning 45

The Internet 47

Internet Bookstores 48

Traditional Bookstores and Libraries. 50

Experts 51

Classes and software 53

The Point of Diminishing Returns 53

Looking Forward. 54

Chapter 6   How to do Projects and Achieve Objectives 55

The Basics of Projects and Objectives. 55

One Final Point—The Hidden Resource 61

Conclusion 62

Looking Forward. 62

Chapter 7   Critical Thinking Examples. 63

The Needed Vacation 63

An Australian Trip. 66
    Your Australian Vacation 71

Building a Home Patio 73

Conclusion 77

Looking Forward. 77

Chapter 8   Fun with Comparison Studies. 78

Consumer Reports® 79

Creating Your own Comparison Studies 79

Purchasing a Car 82

Reviewing Comparison Studies. 91

Doing Your Own Comparison Studies 91

Looking Forward. 92

Decision Making **93**

Chapter 9   How to Make Wise Decisions. 95

What Affects Your Decisions?. 95

The Process of Decision Making. 97

More Decision Making Methods .104

   The Pareto Diagram 104

   The Ben Franklin Balance Sheet Close 110

   Thin Slicing. 112

Looking Forward. 113

Connections **115**

Chapter 10   How to Connect with Others 117

We Speak Volumes 117

Key Principles of Good Communication 118

Connections. 119

Looking Forward. 120

Your Future. **121**

Chapter 11   Discovering Your Multiple Intelligences 123

Our Multiple Intelligences 124

Convergent vs. Divergent Thinking 129

Looking Forward. 134

Chapter 12   Creating an Exciting Future For Yourself! 135

The Shape of Things to Come!. 136

Are You Ready for the Coming Changes?. 138

Using Inflection Points to Improve Your Future 139

Passion and Time Urgency 141

Make a Life List and Check it Twice 143

Visioning Your Own Future 145

Finding Alternative Careers and Activities 148

Your Journey Continues! 149

References and Appendixes **151**

References and Notes 153

Appendix A Critical Thinking Vocabulary 157

Appendix B Your Guide to Critical Thinking Concepts 164

Appendix C Figures and Tables. 171

Appendix D Vacation Planning Forms 173

Appendix E Comparison Study Forms 176

Appendix F Illustrations 180

About the Author **183**

Notes **184**

Acknowledgments

I am fortunate to have some great friends (true professionals) who have helped me get this book into print. They all have strong critical thinking skills and helped on several levels.

To my close friend *Ted Risch* who was the primary editor of this book. Ted did an amazing job of helping to make the book readable and bring it to life.

Ted's education is in literature and he has a wealth of experience teaching a wide array of people in the military and in civilian life. That depth of knowledge coupled with his attention to detail and commitment to making this work special has been invaluable to me. Thanks Ted!

To my close friend *Mark Jepperson* who has been a great sounding board throughout the writing of this book. His concepts on critical thinking have helped to embellish the work significantly. Thanks Mark!

To *Taylor Anderson* from *Lance Fairchild photography* who photographed the picture that is used on the cover of this book. I came to Tyler with the concept and he and I worked closely together to come up with the cover. Thanks Taylor!

To my good friend *Alan Rigg* for his suggestion of using a scroll for the sub-title of the book that led to the brainstorming of the cover concept. Thanks Alan!

Introduction

"There is nothing more uncommon than common sense"
—Frank Lloyd Wright

The purpose of this book is to teach you how to ***think critically***. You will be embarking on a journey of discovery. You will learn concepts, methods, and resources to make informed decisions, complete projects, and achieve objectives. You will also learn how to answer questions and solve problems quickly and effectively.

Critical thinking is an art. Like all art, the strength of the work depends on the skills of the artist. You will become the artist who uses critical thinking as a creative palette to accomplish what you strive for.

This book is designed to help you tap into your wealth of knowledge and experience and to strengthen these areas further. It is *A Guide to The Lost Art of Critical Thinking*. Learning strong critical thinking skills is simply *The Re-Discovery of Common Sense!*

Our Most Powerful Strength

Our ability to critically think is the most powerful strength that we possess. It has allowed us human beings to leave the protection of natural caves, to design and build homes, to make complex infrastructures and teach our young. We create beautiful artwork and write countless novels. We have the printing press, the telescope and the microchip. We build astounding land, air and sea vehicles. The quality of life we humans experience as a group exists in direct proportion to our brain power and how we use it.

Much thinking that people do is disorganized, biased, not thought through or forward looking, and hurried. In the absence of experience, reasoning, confidence and education (both formal and informal), people use feelings and intuition as guides to decision making. This often leads to flawed decisions and unwanted consequences in life. Feelings and intuition are critical parts of the thinking process. However, they must to be backed up with knowledge, experience and wisdom.

What are Critical Thinking Skills?

There are many definitions to critical thinking. That's to be expected. Critical thinking encompasses much of what we do when using our brains.

Words like: reasoning, interpreting, observation and more are used to describe critical thinking. Phrases are also used. Some examples are: rational thinking, focused thinking, cognitive process, reflective thought and informed opinions. Other phrases such as: analyzing and evaluating information to derive a judgment are also used.

These are all good and descriptive words and phrases for critical thinking. However, let's ask the $100,000 question:

> **"What useful things will critical thinking do for you?"**

There are three answers to that question.

1. **To make informed decisions**—Making informed decisions is essential in your life. You have to decide on everything from where to have tomorrow's lunch, to what career to pursue. The more you are able to tap into your experiences and knowledge the better your decisions are.

2. **To understand**—Your ability to comprehend is another essential element in your life. You are exposed to a wide array of information from television, the Internet, books, magazines and people.

- Understanding leads to opinions and decision making. For example, by reading about, and comprehending the positions of two political opponents you are better equipped to make an informed decision on how to vote.

3. **To create, invent and discover**—The ability to create, invent, and discover are human traits that exist in all of us. We create beautiful art, writing, music and more. We invent things like the light bulb, the computer and rockets. We discover things like $E= MC^2$, penicillin, and DNA.

   - The ability to create, invent and discover all require decision making. It is an integral part of each process. There are decisions in choosing a project to pursue. Whatever you pursue there are decisions along the path.

Decision making is the common thread that weaves through the most useful things critical thinking will do for you. It is the primary objective of this book. That is why critical thinking is defined as:

> **The ability to make and carry out informed decisions by efficiently utilizing your lifetime knowledge, experience, common sense, reasoning, intuition, feelings, and confidence.**

A secondary objective of this book is to teach critical thinking concepts useful for understanding any worthwhile subject. As an added bonus you will learn how to use critical thinking skills to create an exciting future.

Critical thinking requires the use of self-discipline and self-examination. The rewards are great freedom and the ability to complete projects, achieve objectives and answer questions with confidence. When you take charge of your mind using critical thinking and make sound decisions, you take charge of your life!

Critical thinking is a skill. It will be strengthened by anyone willing to stretch and grow. The brain acts like a muscle. If used, it strengthens. If shunned, it withers.

Why You Need Critical Thinking Skills

Today there is a lack of critical thinking skills in the workplace and in personal lives. Many people don't know how to critically think effectively even though they are capable of becoming strong critical thinkers. Guidance, patience and practice are needed to learn how.

Critical thinking skills are not prevalent in our society simply because we don't teach them enough. Here is what our learning institutions are doing to teach critical thinking skills.

America's Universities

The United States has many of the finest universities in the world. Some of them emphasize and teach critical thinking skills. Unfortunately, many don't. This is evident because too many students attending are not learning the thinking skills they need to be successful.

The American Institute for Research published a new study in January of 2006. It reports that:

More than 75% of students at two year colleges and more than 50% of students at four year colleges can't read or write well. As examples of this, the report states that these students can't effectively:

- Compare credit card offers with different interest rates
- Summarize the arguments of newspaper editorials

It also states that at least 20% of college graduates completing four year degrees, and 30% of students earning two year degrees, have only basic quantitative and literacy skills. These individuals:

- Are unable to estimate if their car will make it to the next gas station
- Calculate the total cost of ordering office supplies[1]

Yet, they are still able to do these things better than the general adult population.

Where Do We Go From Here?

People can learn critical thinking skills on their own through trial and error. However, trial and error takes much longer than if properly taught and coached.

It is painfully clear that most people aren't taught critical thinking skills in a formal manner, or for that matter, in any manner. Critical thinking skills can be learned at any age though good books and from informed teachers, coaches, mentors and parents who care. The younger the students, the better, however, we all need these skills. To help fill the void, this book has been created.

Knowledge, Experience, Common Sense and Critical Thinking

There are three elements to becoming a powerful thinker. Each is important. Together they are an unstoppable combination.

Knowledge

This includes what you learn from books, teachers, parents, coaches, and mentors. Classes, lectures, discussions and self-study give you much of the knowledge you need to be successful.

Experience

There is no replacement for experience in life. As important as knowledge is, it can't by itself prepare you for the challenges faced in the real world.

Completing tasks are part of your existence. They are always different than what you have been taught through books, lectures and other sources. Experience allows you to gain a deeper understanding and confidence in yourself and your approach to new tasks.

Common sense

Common sense is the glue that binds knowledge and experience together. Common sense helps strengthen reasoning, intuition, feelings and confidence. It helps you become a powerful thinker who is able to use the full potential of your critical thinking skills.

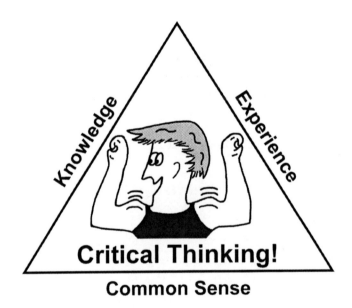

Primary Elements of Critical Thinking

How this book is organized

This book is designed to be used two ways. First, it provides strong fundamentals for critically thinking about any subject. To enhance your learning the chapters are organized in a logical flow and are inter-related. Each chapter builds on the information presented before it. Concepts and methods are provided, questions to stimulate your critical thinking mindset are furnished, and rich examples from history are given. Practical examples are explained step by step using many of the concepts, processes and resources you have just learned.

Second, this book will act as a reference guide. Each chapter teaches a definitive subject and is presented in a clear, crisp and practical manner. Few words are wasted.

I recommend first reading the book from cover to cover. Once you understand the skills involved, the book can be referred to on an as needed basis when you want to refresh your memory about a concept, method, or resource.

There are six sections to this book. The first section is **The Foundation.** It provides you with critical thinking skills. You will understand the essential elements of a strong critical thinker. Next, you will discover the land mines that can stop or damage your critical thinking and how to avoid them. Third, you will learn essential questions to understand the value of information and information sources.

Building on the foundation the second section is **Critical Thinking Methods and Resources.** Its purpose is to provide you with processes and resources to critically think effectively. You will discover methods to solve problems and learn the mysteries of how things work. You will then learn how to use resources to investigate any subject effectively. Third, you will learn a systematic approach to doing tasks. Next, you will be provided with examples to strengthen your skills in doing these tasks. To finish out this section you will discover how to do effective comparison studies.

These methods and resources will prepare you for understanding how to become an effective decision maker.

The third section is **Decision Making.** It brings together the concepts, methods, and resources discussed earlier. It will teach you how to make well informed decisions you can feel good about.

The fourth section is **Connections**. It covers the importance of building strong relationships when involved in critically thinking.

The fifth section is **Your Future**. You will discover your multiple intelligences. Then you will learn the importance of strong convergent and divergent thinking skills. The final chapter will teach you how you can create an exciting future for yourself.

The sixth and final section is **References and Appendixes.** These areas will assist you with the application of the concepts in the book. They include: References and notes, critical thinking vocabulary, your guide to critical thinking concepts, figures and tables, vacation planning forms, comparison study forms and illustrations.

Now, let's get started!

The
Foundation

Chapter 1

Key Elements of Critical Thinking

"Critical thinking is a lot harder than people think, because it requires knowledge."

—Joanne Jacobs

There are many elements to critical thinking. Here are some primary ones:

A Curious and Open Mind

"Millions saw the apple fall, but Newton was the one who asked why."

—Bernard Baruch

A childlike fascination with the world and an open mind about it and the people in it is a powerful combination. Each experience provides one more piece of the amazingly complex puzzle of life. For every challenge undertaken, whether a win or a loss, a success or a failure; invaluable experience is gained. For the critical thinker, education doesn't stop at high school, or college, or grad school, or even after working. Learning is a lifelong commitment.

Florence Nightingale who is best known for her pioneering work in modern nursing was also a noted statistician. In late 1854 she and thirty eight volunteer women went to Scurari (today is Üsküdar in Istanbul) during the Crimean War to care for the wounded. During the first winter there she learned that ten times as many soldiers were dying from illnesses such as typhoid, cholera and dysentery than from battle wounds. She discovered that the hygiene was horrific and the cause of many of these deaths.

After the war Florence Nightingale returned to Britain and used her statistical skills to help write a report to the Royal Commission that outlined the importance of sanitary conditions in health care. She was instrumental in implementing the reports recommendations. Florence Nightingale's curiosity and open mind guided her to improve health care conditions. Her work saved countless lives.[1]

> "Life was meant to be lived. Curiosity must be kept alive.
> One must never, for whatever reason turn his back on life."
>
> —Eleanor Roosevelt

Thinking through Issues

Lower order learning is by rote memorization, associated and drill. Critical thinking encourages digging deeper into issues and challenges. This is done by *thinking through* an objective. Here is one example of how the thinking through process works.

First, facts and data are gathered. Then, assumptions and risks are considered. Finally, an informed decision is made and appropriate action is taken to achieve a goal. This systematically process is known as a *stream of logic*. The more critical the challenge, the more thinking is required.

Flowing Down the Stream of Logic

Sir Edmund Hillary and Tenzing Norgay were the first to successfully climb Mount Everest and return alive. Hillary paid close attention to the smallest details. For example, he invested a full day checking oxygen cylinders and determining flow rates (gathering facts and data). He understood that carefully thinking through their objective could be the difference between life and death. Having enough oxygen to make the round trip would be essential (assumption) because it was critical for survival (risk).

Due to his understanding of the oxygen needs for the journey ahead and always observant, Hillary spotted half-empty oxygen bottles along the way. He decided to pick them up for later use.

After Hillary and Norgay reached the summit of Mt. Everest, they changed their almost empty oxygen bottles with the bottles they had picked up. This got them safely back to camp.[2]

"It is not the mountain we conquer but ourselves."

—-Sir Edmund Hillary

Analyze Issues from Multiple View Points

Almost all issues can be looked at several ways. Different perspectives (also known as view points) help provide better solutions to issues. Common questions to ask yourself are:

- Are there other perspectives that I can view this challenge from?
- What are these other view points?
- How can I use these perspectives to resolve this challenge?
- Am I aware of the cause and effect of any decisions made, or actions taken?

Here is a classic example of an economist who was able to under-standing two different perspectives.

Milton Friedman, a famous economist, was a passionate advocate of the free market. He agreed to debate the hot topic of tuition increase at the state University of California in Los Angeles. The Governor (who was Ronald Reagan at the time) had proposed the increase.

The two viewpoints were clearly opposite. Friedman defended Reagan's proposed tuition increase. The students were against it.

The students were furious at Friedman's position and booed him as he entered. During the debate Friedman turned to the students and called them *"objects of charity."*

In shock, the students listened. Friedman told them that there wasn't another program that clearly transferred income from the poor to the rich as did government subsidized higher education. Tuition reimbursement had "The people of Watts paying for the college expenses of the people from Beverly Hills," he argued.

Friedman understood both viewpoints clearly. This helped him construct a convincing argument for raising the tuition. He knew that no student wanted to pay more money for tuition without a good reason. Friedman also knew that the tuition needed to be increased to be fair to all students, rich and poor. Once the students saw the unfairness of their lower tuitions they voted by a large margin to raise tuition rates.[3]

"There's no such thing as a free lunch."

—Milton Friedman

Opening up to see multiple sides of an issue is a powerful skill. It doesn't mean you have to agree with the opinion of someone else. However, there are frequently two or more views to an issue that are worth considering.

There are significant benefits to looking at multiple view points. You are able to find the best solution to a problem. And, you add to your personal database of alternative solutions and experiences for future problems.

Doing Needed Investigation

To make good decisions, good information is needed. The best way to get needed information is through investigation. An upcoming chapter will explain in depth how to do effective investigation.

Intuitive and Non-Intuitive Thinking

Intuition is a feeling (a sense) that doesn't use rational processes such as facts and data. Good intuition comes from years of knowledge and experience that allows you to understand how people and the world works. Many situations are intuitive. Some aren't.

Non-intuitive things are some of the best opportunities to learn and grow. Book knowledge is important. However, with first hand experience you learn those areas that aren't intuitive. Another term that is commonly used for non-intuitive thinking is *learning the ropes*. Mentors, coaches and teachers work closely with their students to help them learn the non-intuitive (and counter intuitive) knowledge of a subject.

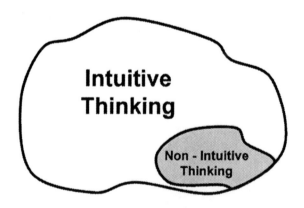

Intuitive and Non-Intuitive Thinking
Figure 1

When working on a task it makes sense to look for the obvious solution first. If the solution doesn't present itself, look for the not-obvious one. And, when attempting to answer a question look for the obvious answer first, then look for the not-obvious one.

Keep in mind, so-called common knowledge may not be correct. Critical thinking works best when you continually ask yourself: Does this make sense? If so, why? If not, why not?

Keeping an open mind to new data and options is another element of sound critical thinking. The critical thinker tests new experiences and knowledge against past experiences and knowledge. If the new experience or information is consistent with what is known, he keeps his view. If not, he strives to learn why there is an inconsistency. Once resolved, he either keeps, or alters his *frame of reference* to account for the new information. A frame of reference includes experience, education, upbringing, culture and many other factors that contribute to how someone views the world.

Here is an example of intuitive vs. non-intuitive thinking. At the end of the example ask yourself: Will this information give me a new perspective? Or, will my frame of reference remain unchanged?

A common statement everyone has heard is: "Buy low and sell high." This seems straight forward; however there is another way of looking at this that is counter intuitive.

William O'Neil, who started a successful financial paper known as Investors Business Daily, says that a more effective way to make money in stocks is to "buy high, and sell higher."

The fundamentals of a company's stock are important. They include things like how financially strong the company is, whether the company's sales and earnings are increasing, whether it is well managed and so forth.

According to William O'Neil, the technical aspect found by studying charts of a stock is equally important. They include price swings, volume, ownership by management and more. These charts reflect the emotions of investors such as greed, fear, hope and despair. Knowing these emotions helps explain dramatic increases or drops in a stock price even when the company seems to have strong fundamentals.

O'Neil feels stock prices are governed in a large part by these emotions. This needs to be taken into account to be a successful investor in the stock market. In other words, stocks that are doing well continue to do well. Falling stocks tend to keep falling.

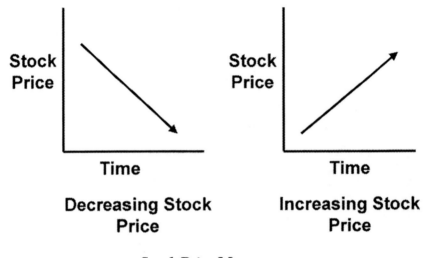

Stock Price Movement
Figure 2

Here is the stream of logic he followed.

Many investors who buy a stock at a high price will hold on to it when it has a significant (sometimes dramatic) price drop. The emotion to "not be wrong" (and sell for a loss) is strong.

A stock may decrease significantly even when the company fundamentals seem to be excellent. Stock swings are frequently indicators that the fundamentals may change in the next several months.

Many stocks that have a severe correction eventually move back up in price—slowly. A high percentage of people sell these stocks when they regain the original price they paid for them. They are happy to get what they put into the stock originally. And, they fear the stock will decrease again.

When this stock reaches a new high, most investors (who were happy to get their money out) no longer own the stock. Then there is minimal downward price pressure.

According to William O'Neil, it might be a good time to buy the stock if it has good fundamentals, fits certain technical patterns and the market is bullish. The stock will frequently move higher quickly.[4] O'Neil has become a successful and well known investor using this philosophy.

Does this reasoning make sense to you? If so, why? If not, why not? What kind of information would you need to question conventional wisdom?

For a concept like this (assuming you haven't heard about it before) to make sense, you would need to do some significant research before changing your mind.

Money is tough to make and easy to lose if one isn't careful. Changing one's beliefs on investing shouldn't be done without doing considerable research.

If a person has held a belief for a long time, a single argument probably won't change his or her belief immediately. This is especially true for any belief that an individual feels strongly about.

This is normal. However, if a new idea or concept sparks a serious question in your mind about what you believe in, then that spark can encourage you to do your own research and learn more. Different reasoning may even change your point of view. This occurs if you find convincing facts and data to back up the new information you have learned.

Other times, you may investigate a subject and are unable to find enough information that convinces you to change your belief. If this happens you will hold to your original belief.

Either way, you haven't taken things at *face value*. This is a strong trait of the critical thinker. This philosophy helps increase your knowledge base.

Discovery of non-intuitive things

There are three ways of discovering non-intuitive things. They are:

a. **Gaining more experience.** Experience is a great teacher. The greater your experience, the easier it is to see the similarity between new ideas and what you learned in the past. Experience teaches you what kind of projects, objectives or problems are straight forward. It also teaches which ones may have non-intuitive (or counter intuitive) issues to address. In other words, experience hones your intuition.

b. **Experimentation.** This can help you uncover inconsistencies. Tinkering is a great way to discover something that isn't consistent with what you thought.

c. **Learning through reading, studying, teachers, mentors, and coaches.** The more you build your base of knowledge, the more you learn about the nuances, differences and subtleties of a wide array of mysteries.

Can Your Critical Thinking Skills be Improved?

The simple answer is yes. We are all different in many ways. Age, gender, IQ, genes, culture, beliefs, life experiences and education are just a few of the factors that make each of us unique.

One of our significant differences is that we all learn at different rates and in different ways. These in themselves aren't important. What is important is the desire and willingness to learn and stretch past your *comfort zone.*

It can be scary to *climb out of one's box* "comfort zone" and view the world with new eyes and ears. However, it can sure be exciting!

This stretching will expand your knowledge base and strengthen your critical thinking skills. The story about the tortoise and the hare is a true to life analogy for developing critical thinking skills. In the long run, persistence and determination will usually win out over raw intelligence that is without direction or desire.

Looking Forward

You have learned the primary elements of being a strong critical thinker. The next step is to understand the land mines to critical thinking and how to avoid them. That is the focus of the next chapter.

Chapter 2

Land Mines to Critical Thinking!

Now, you have a general understanding of critical thinking elements. Next, you will learn some primary threats to successful critical thinking. Let's call these threats *land mines*.

As discussed in the introduction, much thinking of the untrained mind is distorted, incomplete, biased, uninformed and prejudiced. This kind of thinking creates a potential mine field that can hold you back from using your knowledge, schooling, experience, reasoning, intuition, common sense and confidence to make informed decisions.

The purpose of this section is to raise your awareness of the critical thinking mine field and ways of avoiding the mines. Then, you can focus your efforts on thinking more critically.

Land Mines to Critical Thinking

Egocentric Thinking

Egocentric thinking is viewing everything in relation to oneself. Egocentric thinkers are self-centered and consider only their interests. This impedes critical thinking.

It is difficult for many people to identify this characteristic within themselves. The egocentric person is usually unaware of his or her thinking patterns.

There are many successful business people, lawyers, politicians, and others who are egocentric thinkers. They are closed minded to the thoughts and ideas of others. This damages their critical thinking abilities. Open minded thinking is a fundamental critical thinking skill.

The best defense to minimizing egocentric thinking is to be aware of it and to be mindful of the needs of others. In essence, to continually strive towards viewing ideas and concepts from multiple vantage points.

Social Conditioning

Each of us is unique. Age, IQ, race, genes, gender, culture, family, friends, and a wide array of other factors have a dramatic effect on how we view the world and the people we interact with. This conditioning can be a benefit or drawback to your ability to think critically.

Critical thinking is hindered when the world and people in it are viewed from biased social conditioning without learning the needs, desires and dreams of others. It may not be possible to completely understand others, but open minded critical thinking can enable you to listen, learn and empathize. This helps you understand others better.

For example, because someone is a Christian, that doesn't mean he or she can't appreciate the beliefs of Judaism, Buddhism, or Confucianism. The same is true for any religious, social or political belief system.

Arguably the biggest problem in the world today is lack of acceptance. In another word: intolerance. Race, religion, culture, and a wide array of other factors can bring us together or tear us apart. Each of us chooses if we will accept others, or not.

Recognizing and accepting the influences of social conditioning is normal. However, strive to understand how and why they are biasing thoughts. That enlightenment will help clarify your thinking about issues and help guide you towards conclusions that are rational, unbiased, logical and fair.

Biased Experience

Although experience is a wonderful teacher, if it is filtered through a biased or distorted view, that is how it is remembered. Self-delusion supports self-delusion.

Create an open mind and question logic by asking again and again: "Am I thinking logically and rationally." This is called a *sanity check*.

Another good sanity check is choosing friends and colleagues who will tell you the truth, not just what you want to hear. These friends are priceless as *sounding boards* for your stream of thought and rational thinking.

Arrogance and Intolerance

The economist Milton Friedman makes a strong case for individual freedom. He has stated: "The people who always get us into trouble are the people who know better than you do what's good for you." He goes on to say:

> "Arrogance and intolerance are what produce the ills of
> the world."

These simple words say a great deal. When a mind is closed, so is the ability to find the best solution. Critical thinking skills are crippled.

Time and Patience

Time is at a premium. Critical thinking takes time and patience.

Laziness, cutting corners, not doing research and homework can lead to poor decision making. To make the best use of time it is important to focus effectively.

Can you think of a rash decision that you made and regretted later? Did it cost you time, energy and/or money to fix? If you had invested more time thinking about your decision, would you have made a better one?

There is an overused statement at many work places. It is: "We don't have time to do it correctly now, we will rework it later!" This approach costs companies millions each year. It costs individuals dearly as well.

Group Think—The Herd Mentality

There is an old but worthwhile statement:

"When everyone thinks alike no one thinks very much."

It has much truth to it. Critical thinking by its very nature questions ideas, opinions, and thoughts of yourself and others. It uses internal and external reflection.

There are three reasons it can be tough to escape the group think mentality. They are:

1. The group think mentality is present every day from many sources. Radio, television, news papers, magazines and the Internet all reflect the current so called *norm of thinking*. Too many times opinions are stated as fact by self-proclaimed experts. They cater to the most uninformed. Unfortunately, many people don't question what they hear, nor do they question the source of information before repeating it as gospel.

2. The problems of the world are complex. For the non-critical thinker the world is a much simpler place to live.

3. The drive for acceptance from others is a strong motivating factor. Thinking outside the group can be uncomfortable. However, it is necessary for the critical thinker.

Becoming a critical thinker takes conscious and constant diligence. A critical thinker continually asks the questions:

• Does this make sense?

• If so, why?

• If not, why not?

David Crockett was best known for his adventures in the wilderness and fighting at the Alamo. He also served as a Congressman where he was known as an honest and conscientious man.

During the time of his tenure in Congress a law known as the Indian Removal Act in 1830 was being debated. This was a proposed law that would relocate the Five Civilized Tribes of Native American tribes living east of the Mississippi River to further west. It was favored by many who would gain access to lands inhabited by these tribes. They influenced many congressmen.

David Crockett was one of the few in Congress who spoke against the Indian Removal Act. It was passed after a bitter debate in Congress by a small margin and then signed into law by Andrew Jackson.

The relocation of the five tribes had many hardships. It became known as: "The Trail of Tears." Thousands of Indians died during the forced relocation.[1]

David Crockett was a strong critical thinker who followed his own beliefs and values. He couldn't be bribed to support any measure he thought was wrong. His celebrated motto was:

"Be sure that you are right, and then go ahead."

The Drone Mentality

It is easy to fall into a pattern of not paying attention to the world, people and surroundings. This *drone mentality* can sneak up at any time.

Working through daily chores without thinking is one symptom. Another symptom is to shy away from new challenges or problems. Many people live this pattern for years, sometimes decades. Without a conscious effort it is easy to loose critical thinking skills over time.

There are some serious problems to not paying attention to what goes on. The drone mentality can cost dearly.

The movie *Catch Me if You Can* by Steven Spielberg is about a young man who was a brilliant master of deception. It is based on the real life exploits of Frank Abagnale, Jr. who successfully passed himself off as a teacher, a pilot, a doctor and a lawyer all before he reached his 21st birthday! He did this in the late 1960's.

Frank Abagnale, Jr. used disguise and deception to get away with his antics. He passed off bad checks to finance his expensive life by targeting drone like people. He stole the bulk of the money from corporations.

Today, fraud and theft criminals still prey on drone like people however now it is personal. Identity theft and fraud are at epidemic proportions. The scams are getting more creative and damaging.

It is tough enough as a critical thinker to protect personal and private information and not get caught in a scam. A drone like mentality can cost individuals significant time as well as thousands, if not tens of thousands of dollars—or more. Identity theft alone has affected several million people in the United States and is growing.

Always protect personal information. If approached about a "deal" where someone asks for money be very skeptical. Ask:

- Does this deal make sense?
- If so, why?
- If not, why not?

> "What I did in my youth is hundreds of times easier today. Technology breeds crime."
>
> —Frank Abagnale Jr.

Sidestepping the Land Mines

To sidestep the critical thinking land mines first become aware of them. Then, make a conscious effort to avoid them.

Becoming a critical thinker requires continually questioning your thinking and ideas as well as the thinking and ideas of others. This separates you from the crowd. The power and confidence gained by making informed decisions is a worthwhile reward.

Sidestepping the Land Mines

Looking Forward

You now have an understanding of the primary critical thinking elements, the land mines and how to avoid them. To finish this foundation section the next chapter presents critical questions for understanding the value of information and information sources.

Chapter 3

What are some Critical Questions?

The critical thinker has an insatiable curiosity and doesn't take things at face value. Asking questions about information and information sources is fundamental to the critical thinking process. Two critical questions to ask when determining the value of information are:

- Does this information make sense?
- What does my common sense, intuition, experience, and education tell me about this information?

If the answers to either of these questions concern you then learn more about the information and its source. Sometimes you may get a bad feeling known as a *red flag*. This is a clear sign to *dig deeper* to find out about the information and its source(s).

- Red flags often come from past experience or knowledge. Sometimes you get a red flag and don't know why. This comes from experience or knowledge your unconscious mind remembers, but your conscious mind doesn't. Learning to trust and validate your intuition takes time, patience and practice.

- Sometimes information doesn't even pass the *laugh test*. The laugh test is failed when you realize the information is so ridiculous that you know it has to be wrong.

Critical questions help open your mind to look at written and spoken information objectively. The information may be correct. Then again, it may be biased or wrong. By not taking information as fact, just because it has been written or spoken, you begin to discriminate information. This can lead to sound opinions and decisions about the information.

Next, there is a need to continually question:

Information and Information Sources

Information can come from a wide array of sources. Books, magazines, newspapers, experts and the Internet are the primary sources.

What sources can be believed? What information should be discarded?

To help you find worthwhile information and sources ask the following questions:

Where are the best sources of information?

- If the information you are gathering is for general education, finding it on the Internet, magazines, or regular newspapers is usually okay.

- The more critical the information, the more important the sources. Reliable sources can be found in books and articles from established experts, library resources, magazines and newspapers that you have confidence in.

  - You can use unknown sources from the Internet, magazines and articles, but caution is advised. The information isn't governed and a great deal of it is biased and/or wrong. Try to verify information when it is important.

Can the information be verified?

- Finding two more different locations that have the same information is one of the best ways to verify information. Your objective is to find unrelated sources, as information is recopied in many locations today.

  - One way of finding unrelated sources is to look for information that verifies what you are investigating, but is presented differently. This doesn't always guarantee that the source is un-related; however it is a good indicator.

Assumptions

Assumptions about information are crucial. Assumptions are used instead of facts and data when they are unavailable, or time is limited. Wrong assumptions will lead you down the wrong path. Consequently, assumptions need to be questioned.

Ask yourself:

- Are my assumptions valid?
- If so, why?
- If not, why not?
- Do I need to investigate more facts and data?

These questions will help you think through assumptions before using them as "fact." That process helps to screen out bad assumptions. It won't catch all bad assumptions. However, it will catch a good majority of them with practice.

Interpretations and Implications

Continually questioning how you are interpreting (comprehending) information is essential to critical thinking. Some of the land mines to critical thinking such as group think, intolerance or social conditioning can bias interpretations of information.

If you are aware of land mines to critical thinking (as shown in the previous chapter) you can adjust your thinking as necessary. This will help to ensure you are interpreting information accurately and fairly.

Asking a trusted colleague or friend about his or her interpretation of information is a good way to get a *second opinion* to help you to test the validity of your interpretation.

Question the implications of choosing certain information. The more critical the issue, the more important the information, and the more time should be invested in verifying it.

Conclusions

There are several questions that can help determine if conclusions drawn from critical thinking are valid. Ask yourself

- Does the conclusion I came to make sense?
- Does the information I used support the conclusion I reached?
  - If so why?
  - If not, why not?
- Did I ask the right questions?
- Did I ask enough questions?
- Should I review the information, information sources, assumptions, interpretations and implications one last time to be sure of myself?
- Was there more than one possible conclusion?

- If so, did I pick the right one (to the best of my ability) from the facts and data I had to work with? If not, go back to the beginning of this section and start the process over.

Looking Forward

The foundation of critical thinking has been presented in these first three chapters.

In the next section primary Critical Thinking Methods and Resources are covered. The methods and resources explained in these chapters are crucial for the next section of the book which is on Decision Making.

The first chapter in this section will show you how to solve problems and discover the mystery of how things work.

Critical Thinking
Methods and
Resources

Chapter 4

How to Solve Mysteries!

"Everything should be made as simple as possible, but not simpler."

—Albert Einstein

Solving a mystery using critical thinking skills has two meanings. First, it can mean using your critical thinking skills to become an expert in a field. Second, it can mean using a critical thinking method to solve a problem or discover how something works. Let's learn about each of these.

Solving the Mystery

Experts who have solved the Mystery of Their Field

An expert in a field is someone who has a deep and broad knowledge about his or her chosen profession. In other words, he or she is someone who solved the mystery of that field.

One of the elements to becoming an expert is embracing and internalizing a field of expertise. Extensive study, practice, observation and analysis are some of the critical thinking skills that a person applies to become an expert.

An individual who solves the mystery of a profession can frequently replicate those efforts over again. Let's look at a few examples of prominent people who have solved the mystery of their profession.

Warren Buffett has solved the mystery of investing. His success at making money by investing in undervalued companies and then selling them for large gains is legendary. It earned him the nickname, the Oracle of Omaha (Warren Buffett was born in Omaha Nebraska).

Next, Bill Gates is a person who solved the mystery of marketing effectively. He quit college at Harvard to be in the beginning of the personal computer revolution. Today, because of his marketing savvy he and Microsoft are household names.

Third, Steve Wozniak was responsible for much of the early success of Apple Computer. He solved the mystery of making early home computers simple. For example, he found a way on the Apple II to allow the video display and microprocessor share the same memory. He also developed a floppy disk controller that only used a fourth of the integrated circuits used by other controllers at the time.[1]

Solving the mystery of a profession has been explained for two reasons. First, is to show the power of critical thinking when it is applied effectively to a field of expertise. And second, critical thinking skills will be used later in the book to help you decide on the best career for yourself; wherein you may become an expert.

How to Solve Mysteries using Critical Thinking

Below are methods that can be used for doing tasks, solving problems and learning the mystery of how things work. These methods can be used separately, or in combination.

- **The Scientific Method**—powerful, effective and time tested.
- **The 80/20 Rule**—a rough order of magnitude on how the world operates.
- **Tinkering, the Art of Playing**—discovering how things work.
- **Locating the Root Cause of Problems**—discovering this can lead to an optimal solution.

- **Working Backwards**—define results then determine how to get there.
- **Using History as a Guide**—if it worked before, consider using it again.

The Scientific Method

The scientific method is arguably one of the most powerful, if not the most powerful methodology in critical thinking for discovering how things work. For centuries, scientists, engineers, mathematicians, and others have used the scientific method to advance the human knowledge base.

The scientific method uses hypothesis, prediction, controlled experiment, observation, and potential conclusions (possible solutions). With this method scientist are able to discover many things.

For example, Marie Curie helped pioneer the discovery of radioactivity (the detection of radium is considered as the second most important chemical element—oxygen being first). Curie also helped provide the groundwork for nuclear medicine and the discovery of the structure of the atom.

Another example of using scientific method comes from work done in the jungle. Jane Goodall is an English behaviorist who worked with and learned about chimpanzees (Homo sapiens' closest relatives) at the Gombe Stream Reserve in Tanzania Africa. Her discoveries were revolutionary. She was able to show that chimpanzees hunt, approximate language and engage in warfare. Goodall also discovered that chimpanzees make and use tools. Previously, tool making was thought to be a human defining characteristic.[2]

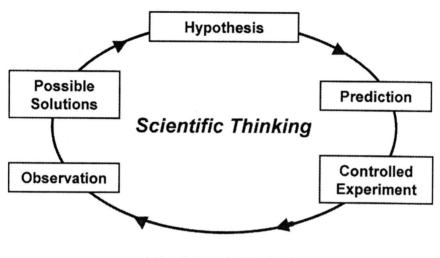

The Scientific Method
Figure 3

Scientists learn from the experiences of those before them. If a new hypothesis (theory) is found to be more accurate than a previous theory, then that new theory becomes the accepted norm. The scientist who came up with the previous theory isn't thought of less. He or she is thought of as having helped other scientists to learn better explanations to the way our world and the people in it operate.

To the true scientist the ultimate goal is to eliminate ego, politics and pride in order to discover the ultimate truths of the universe.

For example, Sir Isaac Newton's explanation of the effects of gravity was accepted as truth until Albert Einstein improved upon Newton's theory and also explained why gravity works the way it does. Einstein's theory of gravity is still the accepted theory for large objects. Einstein used Newton's ground work as his starting point.

Einstein continued his work in physics making major discoveries in relativity, gravity, space, time, matter and energy. For the final decades of his life, Einstein worked on a unified field theory to explain and relate the physical world of the very large and of the very small (quantum mechanics). He never discovered a satisfactory answer to a theory how everything behaves in the physical universe. Eventually someone may. When (if) someone does, that person (or people) will get the credit. However, Einstein did significant groundwork towards that goal.

> "Imagination is more important than knowledge. Knowledge is limited. Imagination encircles the world."
>
> —Albert Einstein

The 80/20 Rule

In the late 1800s an Italian economist named Vilfredo Pareto was studying the distribution of wealth in European countries. He discovered a predictable imbalance in the distribution of wealth. He found that approximately 80 percent was controlled by approximately 20 percent of the population. This was later known as Parato's Principle or *the 80/20 rule*.[3]

The 80/20 rule is an observable natural phenomenon. It governs many scenarios in life in which 80 percent of the results come from 20 percent of the inputs. There is a beauty and elegance to life that repeats itself again and again. The 80/20 rule is one of these rules of thumb that reflects human nature, and how the world operates.

Here are some examples of the 80/20 rule:

- Eighty percent of the work done at a company will be done by twenty percent of the people.
- Eighty percent of the people who fly will be travel with twenty percent of the airlines.
- Eighty percent of the computers will be built by twenty percent of the manufacturers.

- Eighty percent of the music listened to will be created by twenty percent of the artists.

These statements are clearly not exact, but can be made without a great deal of research, and serve as useful guidelines when making general assumptions, or when trying to get a feel for how things work.

Why does the 80/20 rule work so well? The answer is simple. 20% of the people, nature, products and systems stand out (excel) from the rest. Beyond that explanation would probably take many years of research and a PhD dissertation thrown in for good measure. The results probably wouldn't give a much better explanation.

Tasks can frequently be overwhelming. It is easy to flounder if you don't know where to start. The beauty and power of the 80/20 rule is that it can frequently be used to help you determine where to begin.

A question to ask yourself when beginning a task is:

> "Where should I put most of my energies to give me
> 80% percent of the desired results?"

This insightful question will help take a seemingly overwhelming task to something that begins to be manageable. Select the parts of the task (dragons) that will give you the greatest benefit for the least time invested. In other words: Pick your dragons carefully.

Picking your Dragons Carefully

Tinkering, the Art of Playing

Tinkering is the process of playing with something and seeing how it works. This is done by *trial and error*. Tinkering is born out of curiosity and nourished by discovery.

Tinkering is a powerful method because play is all about having fun! There are no goals, no deadlines, no budget constraints, no fear of being wrong—and no pressures. When you play you are at your most relaxed enjoyable state with an open mind.

Tinkering can be simple at times. At other times it can lead to a significant discovery.

Tinkering can be with physical objects such as cars, radios, and computer hardware. Tinkering can also be with a computer program, a completely new dance step in Argentine Tango, or anything else that you can play with and gain knowledge.

Some years ago Dr. Sugata Mitra a computer scientist and head of research and development in New Delhi India had an idea. He wondered what would happen if poor children were allowed unlimited access to the internet.

Sugata launched what became known as the *Hole in the wall project*. He placed a high speed computer with Internet capability in the wall of a slum outside his office and waited to see what would happen. There were no instructions and no teaching, just a computer hooked to the Internet. Trial and error were the only things available to the youngsters who came upon this strange device.

Curious children immediately gravitated to it. They quickly figured out how to point and click, and how to access the Internet and explore. They soon figured out the fundamentals of computer literacy.

Sugata duplicated his experiment several times in different locations. Each time, the children who tried out the computers became computer literate just by tinkering. His experiment verified and re-verified that tinkering and curiosity are powerful critical thinking methods.[4]

The Hole in the Wall Project

Locating the Root Cause of Problems

Some problems have a *root cause* that isn't important to determining an optimal solution. Other times the root cause is important.

Deciding to purchase a house due to an improvement in income and status is a good thing. The root cause of income improvement is nice to know (it means you did a good job). However, knowing the root cause doesn't significantly affect many of the decisions you will make during the purchase of the house. These include selecting a good mortgage rate, options that you want and so forth.

Many problems have root causes that are important to their solution(s). Symptoms are an indicator that there is a problem (or problems) in a business or in one's personal life. The reasons behind those symptoms are important. An illustration is found in the medical profession.

A family doctor is concerned about treating the root cause of a patient's problem rather than the symptoms; otherwise the problem may not go away. If a patient complains of a stomach pain, and the doctor gives that individual an antacid to relieve the pain without doing any tests, then he may only be treating the symptoms. What if the pain was due to an ulcer, or worse?

Medical schools teach a systematic technique to identify a patient's disease causing a patient's symptoms called *differential diagnosis.* A medical condition must be identified before it can be treated. Differential diagnosis is a form of scientific reasoning.

To diagnose a disease, a doctor observes a patient's symptoms by examining the patient and reviewing personal and family history. Then, the physician lists the most probable causes of the ailment. Next, the doctor performs tests to eliminate possibilities until the most likely cause (or causes) for the illness has been uncovered.

Once the cause of the symptoms has been discovered, the doctor prescribes a therapy. If the patient doesn't improve the diagnosis is reassessed and the search for a cure continues.

For example, a patient has symptoms L, M and N. The doctor makes a list of possible diseases that have all these symptoms. This list frequently includes other symptoms. In this case, symptoms P, Q and R are present in certain diseases.

- Disease X: Symptoms L, M, N, and P
- Disease Y: Symptoms L, M, N, and Q
- Disease Z: Symptoms L, M, N, and R

If the doctor can define a test that either verifies or eliminates symptoms Q, P or R he is able to make a strong educated guess on the disease. For example, if symptom R is present, but symptoms P and Q aren't, there is a high probability that the Disease is Z.

This method of thinking using differential diagnosis can be applied to other fields. This is called *transference*.

Sir Arthur Conan Doyle is best known as the creator of Sherlock Holmes. Doyle was a medical doctor in Edinburgh Scotland in the 1880's. The successes of his now classic stories rely on Sherlock Holmes's use of differential diagnosis to solve crimes. Sherlock Holmes would observe many clues, how they were related and then determine who the criminal was. This is an excellent example of transference.

Here is another example of how discovering the root cause of a problem can be the key to solving it.

Malcolm Gladwell explains in his book *The Tipping Point* that it is possible for ideas, messages and behaviors to spread rapidly. Gladwell argues convincingly that to change an entire population it is not necessary to change everyone, only a small percentage of people.

The point at which the ideas, messages or behaviors of a population changes rapidly is known as the *tipping point*. Similar to an epidemic, *contagious behavior* is caused by a small percentage of people.

Wolverine is the company that makes Hush Puppies. They thought about phasing out the brand in the mid 1990's. Sales of the shoes were down and Wolverine thought the shoes were out of fashion. Instead, something interesting happened.

Some young people in New York wore the Hush Puppies, not to make a fashion statement, but because they liked them. They went to clubs and cafes, and walked the streets of downtown New York wearing the shoes. They exposed others to their fashion sense. Sales of the shoes began to rise.

Then, two fashion designers used the shoes to sell something else. The Hush Puppies grew in popularity further. The shoes passed a tipping point of popularity and became a fashionable item for teenagers. The contagious behavior of the teenagers had spread like a virus. Sales of Hush Puppies exploded over the next couple of years.

Changing others by using contagious behavior has significant implications. Much can be accomplished by focusing efforts. Instead of trying to change an entire population, only a small percentage of people need to be convinced to change.

In another story about a tipping point, Malcolm Gladwell discusses how behavior of criminals in New York City was changed. This was done by understanding human behavior and implementing tactics to improve it.

In the 1980s and early 1990's the poor neighborhoods of Brownsville and East New York and their streets had every conceivable violent and dangerous crime. Crime was spreading like a virus. To combat it New York needed a stronger vaccine—in essence, an anti-crime preventative.

A common solution for lowering crime is adding more police and jails. However, this only treats the symptoms of the problem. It does nothing to address the cause of crime nor does it lower it.

To solve its crime situation, New York City implemented what is now known as the *Broken Windows theory*. It was the brainchild of James Q. Wilson and George Kelling. Their Broken Windows theory states that if a window is broken and left un-repaired then people walking by will assume no one cares and no one is in charge. Graffiti, public disorder and aggressive panhandling are the equivalents of broken windows. They were evidence of the virus that was inviting more serious crimes in New York City.

In other words, when a place is messy, people add to the messiness. That was the root cause of the crime in New York City. The solution that the Broken Windows theory provided was to clean up the city. Then, people would have an inclination to keep it clean. That in turn would reduce the serious crime. The discovery of this simple solution has some startling implications.

The Broken Windows theory solution was put into effect in all of New York City when Rudolph Giuliani became mayor. He appointed William Bratton as chief of police. Both Giuliani and Bratton believed that by controlling the minor and seemingly insignificant quality-of-life crimes they could create a Tipping Point for dropping the crime rate.

Giuliani and Bratton executed a policy to fix all broken windows, stop panhandlers, and paint over graffiti. They literally had the streets cleaned up.

For example, Bratton's police officers arrested people for not paying their train fairs. Although a small crime, these actions sent a signal to the criminal community that crime (any crime) wouldn't be tolerated by the authorities. The offenders were taken to police stations and checked for other outstanding offenses. Seven out of ten had outstanding offenses against them.

In another example, when gang members painted their graffiti overnight on trains, the authorities had the trains re-painted by the next morning. The gang members saw their hard work created overnight eliminated. This helped break their will to paint graffiti.

The broken windows theory worked. Crime dropped precipitously. People started caring; they felt someone was in charge. They began taking better care of their city.[5]

Before   **After**
The Broken Windows Theory

Working Backwards

Working backwards means visioning what you want, determining the steps needed to get there and then implementing them.

George Washington was head of the Continental Army during an eight year war that led to the independence of the United States. There were many problems with the army such as insufficient troops, arms, and munitions. Many of the soldiers went unpaid. These problems lead to a high desertion rate.

To defeat the British, Washington would require respect from his troops. Military troops respond well to a strong and respected leader.

To gain the respect of his troops Washington determined he must first gain respect from the British military. If they respected him, then his troops would.

Washington was already known as a gentleman by the British. However, to gain further respect he insisted on being addressed in all letters from the British as General Washington. If a letter wasn't addressed in this manner, he wouldn't accept it. Washington achieved his point and won the respect of the British and of his troops.

The concept Washington used to gain respect from both the British and American troops is called *act as if.*[6]

Let's review:

- Washington's goal was to win the war with the British.

- Washington *worked backwards* to determine to have chance of winning the war with the British he first needed to get the respect his troops.

- Washington acted as if he deserved respect from the British.

- Washington's troops then respected him and followed him into battle with resolve.

- Washington and the Continental Army defeated the British.

> "Discipline is the soul of an army. It makes small numbers formidable; procures success to the weak, and esteem to all."
>
> —George Washington

Using History as a Guide

History is rich with examples that have great ideas on how to approach (or solve) many problems. The old saying *why reinvent the wheel?* is useful.

In an article about a great designer the writer asked him how he designed such amazing things. He answered that he would research thoroughly what he was attempting to design. His investigation usually showed about 95% of what he was designing was already completed. He would then design the remaining 5%!

We accomplish the most when we stand on the shoulders of others.

Looking Forward

This chapter has covered critical methods to solve problems and to learn how things work. In the next chapter you will discover how to effectively use resources to investigate any subject.

Chapter 5

How to Investigate any Subject

The focus of this chapter is how to investigate any subject quickly and easily. Learning how to do good investigations can be enjoyable and rewarding for the following reasons.

- **Doing good investigation leads to better decisions:** Better decisions lead to better results in life. Better results in life leads to a happier life. It's that simple!
- **Investigation leads to learning new things:** Learning something new is exciting and fun because it is a discovery process.

Just in Time Learning

There are many useful resources to help you investigate. The primary ones are: the Internet (including virtual bookstores), traditional bookstores and libraries, experts, classes and software.

To locate information when investigating use *data mining*. You have to sift through a great deal of information to get the golden nuggets of information you seek. Effective data mining invests your time in order to learn what you need to know, when you need to know it. This is known as: *just in time learning.*

There are vast amount of information available on the web, books, magazines and more. Here are some questions worth asking.

- How do you quickly find the best information available?

- How do you keep from going into *information overload?* Information overload is when you feel buried in information and have difficulty knowing what to do next.

- How do you keep from going down *blind alleys* that take you in a direction away from the information you are looking for?

- How do you keep from getting *wrapped around the axle?* That is to say; how do you avoid looking at the same information again and again expecting it to yield something useful when it has little that you need?

Here are some ways to use resources effectively to answer these questions.

Investigating!

The Internet

The Internet is a vast, useful resource. There are ways to get what you need simply and quickly. The following method with help you avoid information overload, blind alleys, and getting wrapped around the axle.

Use a search engine to locate useful information by selecting descriptive words and phrases. For example, to investigate a home project like building a wood patio in the backyard, use search words and phrases like: patio, backyard patio or patio deck. More descriptive phrases improve results. You could use: Wood patio decks, or building a wood patio.

Search engines frequently show thousands of results (hits) for topics searched. This can be overwhelming. However, you will use your time effectively if you take a systematic approach to investigating information.

The first one to three pages of search results will provide you with the most useful web addresses for the search words used. Search engines sort information by relevance to a subject by using a proprietary *algorithm*. An algorithm is a procedure used for solving a problem.

Double click on the web addresses that have the most useful looking information associated with them. Read the first paragraph or two of information on the website. If the information is helpful and easy to understand, read further. If not, hit the back key to get to the search results. Then, double click on another interesting looking web site that was brought up by your search.

Continue the process of reviewing the interesting looking websites. When useful information repeats itself two or three times take note. It is a sign you've located a source of important information for your investigation. Bookmark the pages on the websites that have useful information so you can go back later if needed. Or, print out a copy, if that is your style.

Some information will identify other sources on the subject. If you need more information, these are good places to research next.

How deep you investigate a subject is up to you. It is a matter of interest, need, motivation and time.

Internet Bookstores

If web searching doesn't provide enough information for your investigation, consider purchasing a book or two on the subject.

For any subject there are several ways to locate good books. You can find references to books from websites, magazines and other books on the subject. Also, search for books in the Internet book stores—sometimes called virtual bookstores.

Amazon.com® and Barnesandnoble.com® are two good internet bookstores with descriptive rating systems as follows. These rating systems have four metrics (measurement of usefulness) that are helpful.[1] They are:

A star rating system

The number of stars tells how customers rate a book. There are five stars available (or dots) from these websites. Zero to two star means customers didn't like the book. Four to five stars means customers thought the book was excellent. Look for books that average at least four stars. This indicates the book met the needs of most people who read it.

The number of reviews

The more reviews the better. Reviews are written by people who feel strongly about a book, either positively or negatively. A lot of reviews indicate a book that provided helpful or stimulating information to others. Amazon.com® has the number of people who found the review helpful at the top of each evaluation. Reading these reviews first will save you time.

Sales rank

Review the book's sales rank provided by Amazon.com® and/or Barnesandnoble.com®. This tells how well the book has sold in comparison to all of their books. Compare the sales rank number to other same subject books. More books sold indicate a popular and helpful book.

Book excerpts

Read book excerpts if they are available. If you find that the excerpts have useful and easy to understand information, then the book is a good choice. If not, look for other books on the subject.

This rating system method is a simple comparison study. It will help you determine which book(s) will give you the best information for your time invested.

Sometimes web search provides enough information about a book to purchase it from the web. Or, you may want to study the book more before deciding to purchase it. Bookstores and libraries are good resources to use next.

To investigate a book further, print out a copy of the book's description from the web bookstore, or write the name of the book on a sheet of paper. Take this information to a bookstore or library for further investigation.

Traditional Bookstores and Libraries

Web bookstores only allow you to browse selected excerpts. In contrast, traditional bookstores allow you browse book(s) in detail that interest you before buying. The section in the bookstore that carries the topic you are exploring will have other books on the subject matter. As with browsing in the web bookstores, look for a book (or books) that provides information that's helpful and easy to understand.

Talk to a bookstore employee about the subject you are researching. However, not all employees at bookstores are knowledgeable. To find those who are, go to the information desk. If there isn't an information desk, then locate a knowledgeable individual by asking employees who would be the best person to help you find information about the subject matter you are researching. Then, consult with that individual.

Public libraries are also great resources. The process of finding books is done by researching the subject on their computer system. Libraries have well trained helpful people at the resource desks who will also assist you with your investigation.

Experts

Experts are important resources on their subjects. Two types of experts are top experts in their field and local experts.

Top experts in their field have an almost encyclopedic knowledge of a particular subject. Sometimes there is one person who is considered the best in the field. Most times, there are a few who are better than the rest.

An outstanding example is Peter Drucker. He is a famous business management expert. Many of his concepts are essential parts of American business management practice. If a person wanted to learn about business management but only had time to read a few books, a good choice would be one of Drucker's books.

Here's another example. In the early 1980's I started a screen printing business out of my home. I purchased a book called *How to Print T-shirts for Fun and Profit* by Scott Fresener and Pat Fresener. It was the best "how to" book I have ever purchased. With this book I started a part time screen printing business; and for a while, a full time business. I had the business for over a year.

The book taught me how to build a screen printing business from the ground up, the equipment to purchase and how to price and market the products. It also showed me where to buy shirts, caps, inks and other supplies. It was only 175 pages long, but was full of ideas, resources and illustrations. Few words were wasted.[2]

Selecting a top expert to teach you is a good use of time. Other perspectives are worthwhile; however, learning from the best provides a solid foundation of subject knowledge to build on. Then, if time permits, get different perspectives.

Finding top experts is straight forward. A web search result on a subject for books and articles commonly identifies experts in the subject. When a name continually shows up, take notice, that person is probably an expert in the field.

If an expert has written a book (or books) on the subject, review the book(s). Do a web search on an expert to provide helpful information about his or her experience and background. You may also find that there are articles he/she has written on the subject. Review those as well.

Other resources to locate experts are bookstores and libraries. Go to the section that lists the topic you are investigating. Review books that are helpful and easy to understand.

Many top experts write to others in their field, not to the general public. Understanding their material can be difficult. In this case there are two options to learn about the subject.

First, look for another top expert in the field. If another expert's book explains a subject more clearly to you; select his or her book.

Second, look for *interpreters*. An interpreter is a person who can explain difficult subject matter by restating it for people who want to learn about it, but aren't in that particular field.

Einstein's work on relativity is tough to understand especially for the general public. Fortunately, there are many good interpreters who have studied his work and restated it for most people to understand.

Another example of an interpreter is Thomas Armstrong. He wrote a book called *The 7 Kinds of Smarts*. The book teaches seven different types of human intelligences. It interprets the work of Howard Gardner for the general public.

Gardner's book: *Frames of Mind-The Theory of Multiple Intelligences* is an academic study primarily written for experts in his field. Although good, it can be tough to read for people outside the field.

There are **local experts** for a wide array of subjects. They can be located at businesses and stores. For example, if you are planning on doing a home tiling project, talking with some of the experts at local stores will be helpful.

Seeking out people who have significant experience and knowledge is worthwhile. Ask for the individual at a store or business with the most experience on the task or project you want to do. Then seek advice from that person.

Classes and software

Classes (from community colleges, adult learning and training programs) and software are available to teach various subjects. For exploring subjects in depth consider them as resources.

The Point of Diminishing Returns

Let's return to the questions asked earlier in this chapter:

- How do you keep from going into information overload?
- How do you keep from getting wrapped around the axle?
- How do you keep from going down blind alleys?

Finding the resources available effectively has been addressed in this chapter. This will help minimize information overload, getting wrapped around the axle and blind alleys. Here is another concept to consider that will decrease the effects of these problems further.

There comes a time to move to another step of a project, objective, problem, or to make a decision. This occurs when your time and energy generate minimal useful information. This is known as: *The point of diminishing returns.*

Another way of thinking about the point of diminishing returns is as the opposite of the 80/20 rule. As discussed earlier, the 80/20 rule states that 80 percent of the results come from 20 percent of the inputs. The point of diminishing returns can be thought of as when 80 percent (or more) of your efforts are producing 20 percent (or less) of what you are attempting to accomplish. The point of diminishing returns is a personal decision based on knowledge, experience, reasoning, intuition and common sense.

Looking Forward

In the previous two chapters you learned about powerful methods to solve problems and efficiently use resources to investigate any subject. The focus of the next chapter is to apply what you have learned to real tasks.

Chapter 6

How to do Projects and Achieve Objectives

This chapter presents a straight forward process to do simple and complex projects and objectives quickly and effectively.

The Basics of Projects and Objectives

Critical thinking helps you address tasks of any type and size. By thinking through a project or objective, logical and rational alternatives are determined based on facts, data, experience, and common sense. Then, you will make informed decisions based on confidence.

The process for doing tasks has two parts.

Part I: Define your project or objective

Part II: Structure and then complete it

Part I:

Examples of projects are:

- Building a home office for yourself
- Building a home patio
- Putting in home tiling

Examples of achieving objectives are:

- Going on a great vacation
- Purchasing the right car
- Saving enough for your retirement

Part II:

Structuring a task can be challenging. By using the steps noted below you are able to maximize your time and minimize frustration.

When working with these steps, continually ask questions throughout the process. Questions help to ensure a deeper understanding of your mission and how to handle it effectively.

Asking well thought out questions lead to more worthwhile questions. When one question leads to another question after an answer it is called *begging the question*. For example, when you ask the question: "Have I addressed a task similar to this before?" and the answer is "yes", this begs the next question: "How did I do this last time?"

Step 1: Use your past knowledge

Have you encountered this type of task before?

- If so, what did you do then to address it?
- Were you successful in your approach?
- What did you do right?
- What did you do wrong?

Also ask:

- Do you know anyone who has done this task before?
  - If so, talk with that person (or people) and get some advice on how to handle your task.
- Knowing what you know from past experiences, book knowledge and help from others, what can you apply to do the task at hand?

Step 2: Visualize your desired results

Visualizing the desired results helps you focus on what is needed to address your mission. By determining the desired results you can work backwards and determine the steps needed to get the desired results. Ask the following questions:

- What outcome do you want?
- Is this outcome realistic?
- Why?
- Why not?
- What steps (working backwards) can you take to get this result?

Discussing your desired outcome with friends, family or coworkers can be helpful to clarify what you want to achieve. Others can frequently spark ideas and ways of looking at things that you may not have thought of yourself.

Step 3: Frame your project or objective

Sometimes the most difficult part of doing any task is deciding where to begin. This part of the process can be simplified by *framing*. Framing means defining what you need to do.

To frame your mission you will need to consider the following:

- **Investigation**
  - How much research will you have to do?
  - Where will you find the information you need?
    - Will you use the Internet?
    - Will you use books?
    - Will you need expert help?

- **Financial**
  - How much will it cost?

- **Time**
  - How much time will it take?

- **Resources**
  - How much help from others will you need?
    - Who?
    - When?
    - How much assistance?
  - Will you need other materials or equipment?
    - What will you need?
    - How much will the material/equipment cost?
    - When will you need it?

- **Consequences**
  - What are the consequences?
  - Are the consequences large or small?

The greater the project or objective the more time should be invested in defining, researching and getting the resources you need.

Checklists

Next, take a clean sheet of paper and write down questions that need to be answered.

This process is similar to making a grocery *check list* of items to buy. You make a list of things needed so you can get in and out of the store quickly. Such a list might include:

- Milk
- Cheese
- Cereal
- Meat
- Etc.

Making a check list for doing a task is also helpful. However, in this case the check list is of questions that need to be answered.

For example, suppose you want to go on a vacation. Use the generic considerations noted earlier to create the following questions.

- What is your budget for the vacation?
- How long can you afford to be gone due to work and other obligations?
- What time of year would you like to go?
- Where would you like to go?
- How will you get there?

As you write down questions this begins your stream of logic. Writing down questions also encourages you to dig deeper, not taking things at face value and investigating further. For example, the first question: What is your budget for the vacation?, begs the questions: How much is in your savings (or checking) account that is available for a vacation? Are you willing to put the vacation on your credit card? If so, how much?

Step 4: Collect the facts and data

Next, determine the resources you will need to investigate your mission. Use the resources noted in Chapter 5: How to Investigate any Subject.

Step 5: Determine your available options

Once you have collected the facts and data you can come up with several potential options.

Step 6: Pick a solution and implement

After collecting the facts and data, select a solution and implement it. Sometimes the solution is obvious. Other times you have to do a comparison study.

Note: Comparison studies will be taught in the upcoming Chapter 8: Fun with Comparison Studies.

Feelings, emotions, intuition, past history and the magnitude of your solution may hold you back from deciding. Strive to keep procrastination to a minimum.

Step 7: Modify or change if required

You may require more than one attempt to get a good solution. Consequently, after implementing your solution you may need to modify it. Sometimes significant changes may be required.

Only after applying a solution will you know if the results are what you desired. If it becomes obvious that you didn't make a good decision, rethink it and choose a different solution if possible.

The toughest part of changing any decision is the admission that we are human and make mistakes. In our society many people are schooled to think that mistakes are failures. In reality, mistakes are an important part of the learning process. We all make mistakes, no matter how hard we try. Getting over them, admitting the errors and getting on with improving our decisions is crucial to critical thinking and decision making.

> "Anyone who has never made a mistake has never tried anything new."
>
> —Albert Einstein

Step 8: Review your lessons learned

Each new project you do, or objective you achieve provides you with more experience. This experience is invaluable for future undertakings.

Think about the *lessons you learned*. Ask yourself:

- What went right?
- What went wrong?
- What would you have done differently?

Consider other ways you could have handled your mission that would have given you similar or better results. If this was a difficult situation to resolve consider writing it (and the solution) down on paper or in your computer. You can study this information in the future for ideas if/when you encounter a similar mission.

One Final Point—The Hidden Resource

There is one more resource worth mentioning when doing a project or achieving an objective. The *subconscious* is a hidden resource that can be helpful when critically thinking.

Frequently you will encounter a large barrier when you are working a task. When this happens it is easy to become frustrated. Sometimes this leads to giving up.

Instead, use the hidden resource of your subconscious to help you through these sticky points. It doesn't always work, however it is another useful critical thinking method. To allow the subconscious to work; do the following:

- Don't think about the project or objective for awhile.
- If it's later in the day, get a good night sleep.

Your subconscious is continually working—even when you are sleeping. Have you ever had a project or objective you were having difficulty with and then slept on it? Has the solution ever come to you in the morning? This was your subconscious working for you while you were resting!

Difficult projects or objectives take significant time and energy to complete. Both the conscious and unconscious mind can work in concert to make your efforts successful.

Giving yourself permission to put aside a difficult task away for awhile (assuming you are not under a time constraint) can be helpful. Frequently, you later will get renewed energy to work on your task.

Conclusion

Using steps just learned you can address a wide array of projects or objectives. For simple ones some of the steps may be need little thought, or may be eliminated. For complex ones, the steps will require significant work.

Looking Forward

Now that you have learned a method to do projects and meet objectives it is time to exercise your abilities. That is the focus of the examples in the next chapter.

Chapter 7

Critical Thinking Examples

The last chapter taught a methodology to achieve objectives and do projects. This chapter provides some practical examples.

Two examples are given. The first explains how to plan a vacation (objective). The second explains how to do a home project.

The Needed Vacation

We all need and enjoy vacations to relax, have fun and recharge our batteries. This example illustrates how to get the best vacation for the most reasonable cost.

The method to plan a vacation shown here is applicable to any type of vacation. For example, it can be used for a weekend getaway or a multi-week vacation to any place in the world.

Doing investigation and having flexibility in your schedule are both important to keeping vacation costs down. The prices for airline fares, hotels, restaurants and other travel costs vary widely. With proper research you will be able to locate relatively low cost, high value deals.

Part I: Define your objective

The objective is to take a vacation.

Part II: Structure and then complete it

Step 1: Use your past knowledge

Each vacation is different. Each will present new challenges in having a satisfying time away from home and work. The determining factors for taking most vacations are financial and taking time away from a job or other obligations.

Step 2: Visualize your desired results

The primary benefits will be having an enjoyable vacation, to relax and explore a new location.

Step 3: Frame your objective

Begin by writing a list of questions a check list of things you need to know in order to have a good vacation. This will start your logic stream and will lead to more questions. Questions should be focused on the following areas: finance, time, research, resources and consequences. Ask:

- What is your budget for the vacation?
- How long can you afford to be gone due to work and other obligations?
- What time of year would you like to go?
- How much research will you need to do?
- What resources will you need?
- Where would you like to go?

Step 4: Collect the facts and data

Answer the questions from the list in Step 3.

- What is the budget for your vacation?
  This is a decision based on income and lifestyle and should be determined before taking a vacation. This is true unless you are one of the rare few where money is not a factor in deciding on a vacation.
  Once you have decided on a budget there are some more questions to ask: Will you save up money for the vacation before taking it? Will you use a credit card or a bank loan and pay back later?
  Once you have decided on a budget, you can develop vacation options using the available money.

- How long can you afford to be gone due to work and other obligations?
  Like your budget, this is a personal question. It depends on work, family and other commitments.

- What time of year would you like to go?
  For many destinations the time of year will govern your costs. Traveling off season can save you anywhere from 20-40% (sometimes more) of the costs.
  Talk with travel agents or airline agents to determine the off season. Then, if you can adjust your vacation schedule to coincide with the off season you can save significant money.

- How much research will you need to do?
  It can take a month or more of investigation to plan a vacation.

- What resources will you need?
  The Internet and bookstores are good places to locate most of the information you need to plan a vacation. As noted ear-

lier, travel agents and/or airline agents can be helpful in your investigation.

Step 5: Determine your available options

Continue answering the questions noted in Step 3.

- Where would you like to go?
  Determining a vacation destination is another personal decision. The best way to decide on a vacation is to sit back, relax, have a cup of tea or coffee and daydream for a little while.

The possibilities are endless. Ask yourself:

- Where have I always wanted to go?
- What would I like to see?
- What would I like to do?
- Would I like to do some exploring?
- Would I enjoy relaxing on a beach?

The bookstores have a great number of travel destination books for just about any major place on our planet. They can give you great ideas on places to go. The Internet is a good resource for locating vacation spots.

An Australian Trip

For the purpose of this discussion consider a trip to Australia; leaving from central United States. The trip will take one and a half weeks since it is a long distance. Assume you have $3,000 available for your trip.

Since Australia is often visited by people from the US there are many good deals available. There are two options available for an Australian vacation.

Option 1: Take a guided tour

Travel agents have access to many fine tours if you decide to go this route. The agents are informative and helpful. You can choose a tour where you have a lot of free time, or a little. This depends on what you are looking for.

One advantage of a guided tour is that someone else plans the tour. All you need to do is pack, make sure you have home and work obligations taken care of while you are gone, and then show up and enjoy. Another advantage is that you can make new friends on tours.

There are two primary disadvantages. First, a tour may not go to all the places you desire. If you are someone who likes to do your own exploring, or go to out of way places, tours may not be right for you.

Second, with a tour you don't get to choose your fellow traveling companions. Sometimes there are people with whom you might not enjoy traveling with.

Option 2: Design your own vacation

To design your own vacation, use the web or visit bookstores to start your investigation.

Start researching on the web by typing the phrase: "Australia vacation" into a search engine. Other phrases like "Australian travel" will work as well.

Purchase one or two guide books from a book store and design your own vacation. It is a good investment to purchase one or two travel books for your vacation whether you design your own vacation, or go on a tour. Travel books pay for themselves several times over again. They are filled with inexpensive but nice places to stay, travel tips, where to find bargains, and the best places to visit. Many also include worthwhile information about the history and culture of the area.

Note: Two travel books are usually better than one for long vacations to far away places. This is because each will have different information and various deals that are difficult to find with only one source.

Looking through the various guides at a book store is the best way to select the travel book(s) that will meet your needs.

Step 6: Pick a solution and implement

I will use option two to illustrate how to design your own vacation. Assume a ten day visit to Sydney Australia. It is a large city with many sights to see.

Plan on traveling for three days (there and back). You will stay in Sydney for seven days and eight nights. For the purposes of this example you will travel with one other person. This will help you save on hotel costs and provide you with companionship. Here are the primary expenses for the vacation.

The dominating costs for vacations are: travel, hotel expenses, food, excursions, gifts and souvenirs. Depending on your planning budget, there are a number of opportunities for savings. Let's look at each of these separately.

Travel expenses

- **Flying**—Airline tickets can vary in price by 100-200% or more in cost. Comparison shopping can help you save significant sums of money.

  Airline tickets are less expensive during the off season. This is especially true for international travel. You will usually find better rates if your vacation schedule is flexible. To find out when the off season is (and the rates) for a particular location, talk to an airline agent(s), or travel agent(s).

  International traveling is often the best use of frequent flier miles. The number of frequent flier miles required for an international flight ticket is a better bargain than using miles for a domestic flight. For example, I recently took a trip to South

America during the off season using 40,000 frequent flier miles. The cost of the ticket would have been well over $1,000.

☺ Note: When you are traveling to a destination that has a stopover in a place that is of interest to you, ask the airline agent if you can stay for a couple of extra days. If allowed, you will be able to fly to two destinations for the price of one!

This method worked well for a friend and me in late 2005. We traveled to Cairns Australia for a dive vacation with a stop over in Sydney. We asked; and were allowed to stay in Sydney an extra day without paying extra for the stop.

• **Rental cars**—Once you get to your destination you may need a rental car. They can be found though an Internet search or using the phone book.

Renting cars internationally is not recommended for someone who hasn't traveled much abroad. Insurance, laws governing driving and different driving patterns can be both dangerous and stressful for the visitor. It is best to use trains, planes, buses, and taxis until you are comfortable with driving in the area.

Hotel expenses

As with airline tickets; the difference in hotel prices can vary by as much as 100-200%, or more. The off season rates also provide many saving opportunities.

Selecting a hotel in a central location can save costs on taxi, bus and train fares. Investigation once again is the key to finding good deals. A first priority should always be locating hotels that are clean and safe and in a decent part of the city you are visiting. Hotels like these are known as three star hotels on such websites as Travelocity.com® or Orbitz.com™.

Some hotels charge astronomical prices. Frequently, the only benefit is a mint on the pillow and a paper at the door in the morning. Is this worth an extra $50 to $75 a night—or more?

Consider staying at a bed and breakfast location. Meeting the people who run these establishments and absorbing the atmosphere that embraces the local culture can be an added benefit to your vacation experience. Also, room rates are frequently more reasonable than at hotels.

Some hotels include in the price of the room a continental breakfast or full breakfast. This is good for two reasons. First, the difference in cost of a hotel that includes breakfast is frequently less than the cost of a breakfast purchased outside the hotel. Second, eating at the hotel gives you more time to enjoy the sites and experiences.

Food

There are reasonably priced restaurants in most cities. If you constantly eat at four and five star restaurants you will pay much more. This will increase the price of your vacation. Eating at nice, but inexpensive restaurants can save on vacation costs considerably.

Having said that, it is important to relax and enjoy your stay; one or two nights at a special restaurant won't change the overall cost of your vacation significantly—and, it will be an added treat to your vacation.

Excursions

Excursions are a great way to visit and learn about various areas. The costs of excursions in comparison to the other costs of travel are usually reasonable.

A word of caution: Some excursions aren't worth your time or money. Check with an informed hotel staff member if you are unsure of the quality of an excursion(s) you are considering. Many times he or she will be able to direct you to the best one(s).

Gifts and souvenirs

Buying gifts and souvenirs are not usually primary expenses of most vacations. However, you may want to consider doing some of your birthday or Christmas shopping while on vacation. Many people enjoy getting a thoughtful gift from a far away place.

Your Australian Vacation

For an Australia trip at the time of this writing a discounted fare of $1,330 to Sydney from the central United States during the off season was available.

The average price of good, inexpensive, clean and safe hotels in Sydney at the time of this writing were in the range of $90-$150 US dollars including tax. You could select a hotel for $120/night. That includes a regular breakfast at the hotel you stay at. You will be sharing with a friend so your cost is $60 average per night.

Your food costs will only be for lunch and dinner. Allocate $65/day. By being conservative on your food bills for most days you will have enough extra money for a couple of evenings at high end restaurants and keep within your budget.

This plan includes taking four excursions found on the web. The average cost allocated is $70 each. These are day trips to some outlying areas.

Allocate $320 for gifts, souvenirs and miscellaneous expenses, to complete your trip expenses.

It is smart to lock in the plane fare and hotel prices as soon as you are sure you are going on a vacation and have firmed up the dates. Otherwise, you might be shocked to discover a cost increase of several hundred dollars for a trip like this one. The closer to the trip time you are, the fewer seats will be available on international flights, and the availability of inexpensive good hotels will decrease.

This spreadsheet shows your expected expenses.

Activity	Cost per day (each person)	Number of days	Number of days	Number of excursions	Average cost per excursion	Total expected cost
Travel Expenses						
• Airfare to: Sydney A.						$ 1,330
• Car Rental						$ -
Gas						$ -
Hotel Expenses (Inc Tax)	$ 60	7				$ 420
Food	$ 65	7				$ 455
Excursions				4	$ 70	$ 280
Gifts, souvenirs, Etc						$ 120
Miscellaneous Expenses						$ 200
Expected costs						$ 2,805

Australian Vacation Planning Form
Table 1

Note: A blank vacation planning form similar to the one shown above is provided in **Appendix D** so you can do your own vacation planning.

Step 7: Modify or change if required

No modifications to your original plan are needed.

Step 8: Review your lessons learned

Using the investigation noted above for your Australian trip, you can expect to be under your original budget. Here is an example of some expected lessons learned from this example:

- You saw a great city in Australia.
- You went on four excursions around the city for a reasonable amount of money.
- You saved 30–40% than if you had not been careful with the planning by:
  - Flying during the off season
  - Doing the proper investigation to locate a good clean, safe and reasonably priced hotel in a central location
  - Sharing hotel costs with a friend and companion
  - Eating at reasonably priced restaurants most evenings

Building a Home Patio

This example shows how to do a project

Part I Define your project

In late 2002 I purchased a home in Tucson Arizona. The backyard had a wonderful view of the city lights. Unfortunately, they could only be seen when standing up. I thought that it would be a worthwhile project to put in a patio where friends and I could enjoy the evenings with city lights in the background.

I decided to build the patio myself. It seemed like an enjoyable project to do and I would learn a new skill. I expected to save a good deal of money on the labor costs.

The primary impacts of the decision to build the patio were:

- Cost of the patio
- Property Improvement—a potential financial gain when I sell in the future
- The expected emotional satisfaction and pride of learning a new skill

Part II Structure and then complete it

Step 1: Use past knowledge

I had never built a patio before. However, when I was growing up I was fortunate to have a father who often built things around the house.

My father built a patio out of pavers, a wooden swing set and other things. He wasn't afraid of doing new projects. He would research a project until he understood how to proceed. Then he would do it. I was lucky; some of his skills rubbed off on me.

Step 2: Visualizing the desired result

I wanted an attractive patio large enough to comfortably accommodate at least 6–10 people.

Step 3: Frame the project

I made a check list of questions to determine how to build a patio. These questions led to other questions. Here are a few:

- Where do I get the best information about building the patio?
- What should the patio be made of?
- How large should the patio be?
- How much time will it take to build the patio?
- How much money can I afford to pay for the patio?

Step 4: Collect the facts and data

I had never built a patio before so facts and data were needed. In Tucson Arizona the patio needed to be designed to withstand hot dry summers.

I picked up two good books on building patios at a local home improvement store and read them cover to cover. They gave me different options to consider and had many illustrations. I studied the books and my property to determine what the patio should be made of, the size, how much time it would take to build, how much money it would cost and so forth.

Next, I went to businesses that carried patio construction supplies (pavers, cement, wood etc). I asked local experts a lot of questions, and studied displays and materials.

Finally, I contacted a colleague and friend who is a trained architect. He helped me by answering many questions throughout the process of building the patio.

Step 5: Determine the available options

I considered several different types of patios. The three most promising options were either made of wood, cement, or of pavers. I studied the cost, ease of fabrication, the durability and the probable maintenance.

Step 6: Pick a solution & implement

I selected pavers for the top of the patio. They would be the easiest to construct, maintain and should last for fifteen years or more (assuming I did a good job—and I was able to do so). My solution called for the base of the patio to be constructed with a large mound of compressed dirt. Rocks were placed on the sides for aesthetics.

Steps to walk up to the patio were constructed from wood railroad ties and bricks. The concept for the steps was found in one of the patio books.

I did all of the primary work by myself. This was a good learning experience and saved me a lot of money. The cost for the entire project was probably about 1/3 of what I would have paid to a contractor. This was good, because like most people I was house poor after purchasing a new home.

To finish off the patio I designed and built two redwood benches from patterns I had found in one of the patio books. I purchased an iron fireplace and a couple of torches for the final touches.

The construction of the patio took about two months of evenings and weekends. It still looks good today.

Step 7: Modify or change if required

The patio needed no modifications after it was completed.

Step 8: Review your lessons learned

- Purchasing books on building the patio was useful.
- Building the patio provided emotional satisfaction.
- Using the critical thinking process to work through the project was helpful.
- Getting help from an architect friend helped solve several construction issues.
- The work strengthened my confidence for doing home projects.

The Finished Home Patio

Conclusion

The steps used here can be applied to many different types of projects and objectives with similar successful results.

Looking Forward

You have learned several methods and resources for critical thinking in the first four chapters of this section. Next, you will discover how to do comparison studies (sometimes known as comparison shopping), the focus of the next chapter.

Chapter 8

Fun with Comparison Studies

"Fortune favors the prepared mind"

—Louis Pasteur

A decision method that compares different products and services to determine the highest quality best value product is known as a *comparison study*. Another phrase for comparison studies commonly used is *comparison shopping*.

You do comparison studies every day. For example, you do a comparison study when you decide to go out to a nice dinner. There are usually several good restaurants to select from. Which one should you choose? Comparisons are usually on: price, location, quality of food, atmosphere and service. By comparing each of these you will decide which restaurant to visit.

Comparison studies can be used to decide on a wide array of choices. They can be used to decide on: what car to buy, where to live, what credit card to select and more.

This section teaches how to set up and do your own comparison studies.

Consumer Reports®

Good examples of comparison studies can be found in Consumer Reports Magazine. Consumer Reports® tests and reviews a wide assortment of products such as: cars, digital cameras, big screen televisions, appliances, printers, computer virus protection, exercise machines and more. Much of the information comes from consumers who rate the products. Consumer reports® assembles this information in an easy to read and understandable form. Their studies compare features of various products. Examples are: make and model, price, quality, reliability, and ease of use.

Consumer reports® gives an overall score for these products. It provides Consumer Reports Best Buy Recommendations. If you are interested in seeing its examples of comparison studies after reading this section and you haven't used Consumer Reports® before, consider picking up a copy of the magazine on your next trip to a bookstore.

Creating Your own Comparison Studies

There are two components composing comparison studies. They are: Subjective components and objective components.

Subjective components are based on personal opinions, feelings, instincts and intuition. Examples of the questions asked when comparing subjective components are: What color do you like; green, red, blue or black? Do you feel a component is poor, fair, good or excellent?

Objective components are definitive. These are measurable and scientific. For example, some of the questions answered in an objective comparison study are:

- Does this component exist (Yes or No)? For example, does the computer come with a flat screen monitor?
- What is the cost of a product? This is sometimes a defined price. Other times it is a price range.

Comparison studies usually involve both subjective and objective components. For example, consider purchasing a LCD television. An objective component would be the price range that the television cost should be within. A subjective element would be the quality/reliability that can be rated as poor, fair, good or excellent.

Comparison studies can be done for a wide assortment of consumer goods and services. A comparison study focuses on primary elements of selecting a product. The steps for doing a comparison study are straight forward. They are:

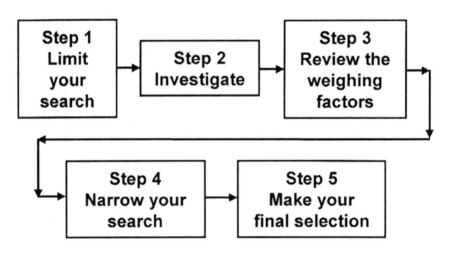

Steps for Doing a Comparison Study
Figure 4

Step 1: Limit your search

Select the factors that are most important to you. This is known as establishing *selection criteria*. Most comparison studies for products and services start with three important factors. They usually are:

- Price
- Quality and reliability
- Usefulness (Utility)

Today there are many options available in a wide array of products and/or services. It is important to have general idea what you are looking for before setting up a comparison study. General reading about the product or service can help you limit your search.

Step 2: Investigate

Use the resources discussed in Chapter 5: *How to Investigate and Subject* such as the Internet, libraries, bookstores, magazines, experts and interpreters for your investigation.

Step 3: Review the weighing factors

A *weighing factor* is the relative importance (ranking) of each factor used in a comparison study. For example; as mentioned; price, quality, reliability and usefulness are usually the most important factors when making a decision on most products or services. Other factors will also need to be considered.

Many items will eliminate themselves because of high price, low quality or lack of usefulness.

Step 4: Narrow your search

After completing your investigation and deciding on the relative importance of the various factors, narrow the search of products or service to a handful of possibilities (options) that meet your needs.

The 80/20 rule can help you narrow the search. Look for the 20% of products that have the highest quality/reliability, highest usefulness within the price range you have decided on.

Step 5: Make your final selection

Set up a comparison study chart for the handful of narrowed down to products. Do a comparison and make a selection.

Purchasing a Car

Let's do a comparison study for purchasing a car. People usually purchase a vehicle several times in their lifetime. It is a good example to illustrate the process.

Step 1: Limit your search

Most people have already decided on the type of car they want before searching for a vehicle. They have determined it will be a family car, or a luxury car, or a truck etc.

Assuming you have decided on the type of vehicle you want, your next task is to determine your selection criteria. Start with: price, quality/reliability and usefulness.

Next, determine other features that interest you and are specific to automobiles. Define these by reading articles in used and new car book and/or magazines. Also review automobile websites. Look for the features that continue to show up again and again. Add these features to your selection criteria.

1. **Price range**—What is your budget for the car? Besides price, cost of a car includes tax, title and insurance costs. This usually adds 10-12% to the base price of the car. Several factors determine what how much can be afforded to pay for a car. The important ones are: What is your income and other current expenses? What is a comfortable monthly payment? How

much can you put out as a down payment? How much trade in money will your existing car provide?

2. **Quality/Reliability**—How important is the quality and reliability of the car to you?

3. **Usefulness (Utility)**—Is this automobile for fun? Is it for a family? Is it for hauling things? How many people will frequently travel in the car?

4. **Looks**—How important are the looks of the car to you?

5. **Gas mileage**—How important is gas mileage to you?

6. **Depreciation**—How fast will the car depreciate? Is this important to you?

7. **Handling**—How easy is the car to handle? Does it take curves well? You will need to test drive it to find this out.

8. **Power**—Do you want a car with a lot of power to get in and out of traffic?

9. **Company**—Is there a particular automotive company that we would prefer to buy from because of past experiences?

Here are other considerations when shopping for a car.

10. **New or used**—How important is a new car to you? Typically, a new car loses 15-25% of its value when it is driven off the lot. The first two or three years usually have high depreciation rates as well.

11. **Trade in or sell**—Do you want to trade in the existing car or sell it on your own? Selling a car rather than trading it in will frequently be worth a thousand or more dollars.

12. **Payments and down payment**—How large are the payments? Do you want to pay the car off in two or three years, or will paying it off in four to six years be okay? Do you want to put the minimum down payment towards the car, or more? The

more you apply towards a down payment, the less the monthly payments will be, or the less time to pay it off (or both).

Now, for this example let's go through the steps to purchase a car. This process will be done for a single man, age thirty four who needs a car. I will name him Jack.

Jack has a good job and would like a sporty car that is attractive. However, he is on a budget. He plans on keeping the car 4-5 years before selling it. Jack would prefer a new car, but will consider purchasing a used one.

Step 2: Investigate

To help learn about available cars Jack purchased two books at a bookstore. One of the books was on new cars, and other one was on used cars. He also investigated on the web.

The books and sites on the Internet taught Jack about the benefits and drawbacks of different makes and models. They educated him about the features, options and prices of new and used cars. After reviewing the books and websites Jack made a list of cars he was interested in.

Jack preferred a new car. After his investigation he discovered that by buying a two or three year old used car (that had a good 80% or more of its useful life remaining), he could save approximately 30-40% off what he would pay for a new vehicle. He decided that by purchasing a used car he would get the most car for his money.

Here are the other factors Jack reviewed and decided on.

1. **Price Range**—Jack determined with his salary and other expenses he can afford $18-22K for a used car 2–4 years old with less than 30,000 miles on it. Jack discovered that a two or three year old car with low mileage was a *sweet spot* for getting an automobile. A sweet spot is when the car has a good amount

of life remaining, however has depreciated enough so that the cost is desirable.

2. **Quality/Reliability**—High reliability is important to Jack. He wanted a car that will last over 100, 000 miles with proper maintenance.

3. **Usefulness (Utility)**—Jack needed a car to drive to and from work, on vacations and around the city. He decided a subcompact or a compact car would be economical to drive and maintain. He was interested in a sporty, but not a sports car (too expensive). Jack likes convertibles.

4. **Looks**—Jack is single and wanted an attractive car.

5. **Gas mileage**—Jack wanted a car that gets a minimum of 20 miles per gallon in the city and 24 miles on the highway.

6. **Depreciation**—Jack wanted a car that doesn't depreciate radically. He felt that if he purchased a reliable car the depreciation should be acceptable. Since he will purchase a reliable used car (2-3 years old) a significant portion of the deprecation has already occurred.

7. **Handling**—Jack wanted a car that handles well in good and poor weather and hugs the road well when cornering.

8. **Power**—Jack wanted a car with good power, however doesn't need excessive power.

9. **Company**—Jack doesn't have a favorite company.

Other Considerations:

10. **New or used**—Jack decided to purchase a used car for the reasons noted earlier.

11. **Trade in or sell**—Jack decided to sell his current car himself (it is an Acura with 129K miles) instead of trading it in. He determined that he was able to make $1,500 more than if he traded it in.

12. **Payments and down payment**—Jack decided he would try to put the money from the sale of the Acura as a down payment. He would then take out a four year loan and start making higher payments so he could pay off the loan in two or three years and save on interest.

Step 3: Review the weighing factors

Jack decided that price, quality/reliability, usefulness and looks were the most important factors in his choice of an automobile.

Step 4: Narrow your search

To narrow his search, Jack invested more time looking through the used car book he purchased along with websites that sell used cars. He read reviews on each of the models and looked at comparison studies that were already completed. Jack narrowed his search to four models. They were:

- **The Ford Mustang Convertible**—Mustangs have good reliability and quality. Jack liked their handling. The used Mustangs were reasonably priced and get satisfactory gas mileage. Jack liked the convertible and found the Mustang's appearance attractive. He located several used cars in his city that were 2-3 years old and within his price range.

- **The Honda Accord**—Jack was impressed with the reliability and quality of these cars. The appearance was appealing to him. The price and gas mileage were reasonable.

- **The Acura TSX**—Jack liked the reputation of Acura. The used cars were reliable, attractive to him and roomy inside. However, the used cars were expensive.

- **The Toyota Corolla**—Jack liked and reliability of the car, and the company reputation. However he didn't feel it was an attractive car.

Choosing the Right Car!

Step 5: Make your final selection

Jack visited several car dealers of the brands noted above. He test drove each of the models. Test driving information is factored into subjective information such as handling, and power.

Jack decided to purchase his car from a car dealer instead of a private individual. He wanted a warranty and inspection report on the car which he could only get through a dealer.

Although Jack liked many features about the Acura TSX, it was more expensive than he felt could afford in comparison to the prices for the other cars. The Toyota Corolla was a good car, but Jack didn't find it attractive. He liked both the Honda Accord and Mustang. He finally decided on the Mustang convertible. Besides the good reliability and price he liked its handling and appearance. He also chose it because it was a convertible.

Below is a comparison study chart Jack created to contrast the cars he was interested in. The columns are filled in using two sources of information. First, the chart includes objective information such as gas mileage and price. Jack learned about these by reading articles and reports in books, magazines and on the web. And second, the table includes subjective information factored in by test driving the cars.

No.	Make & Model	Price Range	Used Car (2-4 yrs)	Quality & Reliability	Utility (Sporty)	Looks	Approx. Gas mileage (Miles per Gallon - MPG)	Depreciation	Handling	Power	Company
1	Ford Mustang Convertible	$18-24K	Y	VG	E	E	20-26	F	G	G	G
2	Honda Accord	$18-22K	Y	E	F	G	30-40	F	G	G	E
3	Acura TSX	$24-29K	Y	E	G	E	22-30	F	G	G	E
4	Toyota Corolla	$17-21K	Y	E	F	P	30-38	F	G	G	E
	Jack's Requirements	$18-24K	Y	VG	G	G	20-24	F	G	G	G

Y =Yes
N= No

P = Poor
F = Fair
G = Good
VG = Very Good
E = Excellent

Jack's Automobile Comparison Study Form
Table 2

The price ranges Jack found most commonly are noted in the table. This can be charted on a figure commonly used in statistics known as a Normal Curve (Also known as a Normal Distribution Curve). A normal curve charts the average cost of each vehicle verses the quantity at that price. It is useful for Jack because it helps him focus his attention on cars within a fair price range.

Jack found prices found outside of these ranges, however they weren't as common. Cars with significantly lower prices usually had been in an accident, or needed significant repairs. More expensive cars usually had an inflated price.

Below is a Normal Curve for the Mustang Convertible that shows Jack's selected price range.

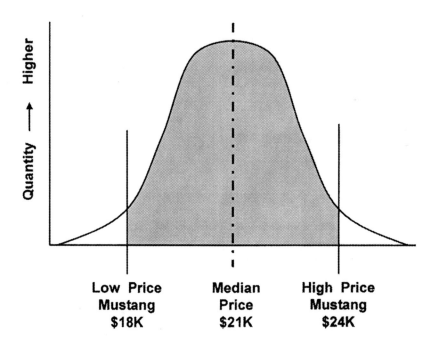

A Normal Curve of Mustang Convertible Costs
Figure 5

Once Jack decided on purchasing a used Mustang convertible, he negotiated with various dealers on the price. To negotiate a fair price, he used comparable age, mileage and options information from used car books, prices he found on the Internet and at the various dealers he visited. Using the comparison study steps shown, Jack was able to successfully fulfill his need for a good, reliable and attractive car.

Reviewing Comparison Studies

Comparison studies have a wide array of uses. For example, they can be used to help make decisions on homes, cars and computers. Comparison studies can also be used to decide on which college to attend, what career to pursue and more.

Before ending this chapter it is worth noting again how to determine the important factors when setting up any trade study. They are:

1. Start with the following factors. They are almost always important.
   - Price
   - Quality and reliability
   - Usefulness

2. Next, during your investigation look for:
   - Features that continue to show up again and again during your investigation
   - Add any other features that are important to you.

Doing Your Own Comparison Studies

Blank forms are provided in **Appendix E** for you to do your own comparisons studies on cars and other products.

Looking Forward

You now have a strong foundation of critical thinking skills. You have learned to use critical thinking concepts, methods and resources. The next step is to apply this knowledge to making wise decisions. That is the focus of the next chapter.

Decision
Making

Chapter 9

How to Make Wise Decisions

"When all is said and done, more is said than done!"

—Lou Holtz

Preceding chapters of this book covered concepts, methods and resources used to make good decisions. This chapter expands that knowledge, and the process for making sound decisions. It also provides more decision making methods.

What Affects Your Decisions?

In the introduction critical thinking was defined as:

"The ability to make and carry out informed decisions by efficiently utilizing your lifetime knowledge, schooling, experience, reasoning, intuition, common sense and confidence."

Decisions come in all sizes and degrees of difficulties. Many are small and insignificant. Others are large and life altering. Most are in between. Your decisions are affected by money, stress, time, facts, data and resources. These factors need to be individually and collectively considered when making decisions.

- **Money**—It governs what you can and can't afford. For example, if you want a $50,000 car, but can only afford a $20,000 car then you will only look for cars in that price range. Or, you must be willing to readjust (or violate) your budget.

- **Stress**—Internal or external pressures can affect your decision making. Although some stress is always present during decision making, it can be managed. If you are under a lot of pressure and time is available, hold off your decision until later. If time is short, then acknowledge that you are under stress and strive to minimize its effects on your decision.

- **Time**—Sometimes there will be adequate time available to make a good decision. At other times it will be limited. You won't be able to investigate aspects of your decision as much as you would like. In these cases you must depend on your current knowledge, experience, schooling, reasoning, intuition, common sense and confidence. In other words; your critical thinking skills.

- **Facts, data and resources**—There are vast information resources available today. The primary ones include: the web, bookstores and libraries, experts, colleagues and friends, classes and software.

Digging deeper into decision making

People who grow as critical thinkers and become good decision makers make it a point to learn from every decision (right or wrong). They are willing to experience new things and learn ideas and concepts with an open mind. Experience and book knowledge coupled with common sense leads to wisdom. Wisdom leads to better and more confident decisions. Better and more confident decisions lead to a better existence in general.

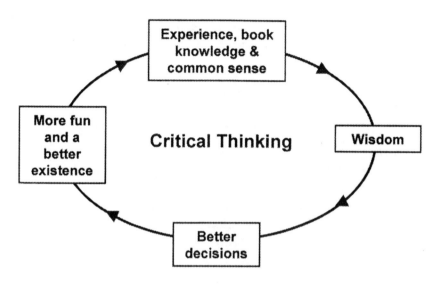

The Decision Making Process
Figure 6

The Process of Decision Making

These are the steps for effective decision making:

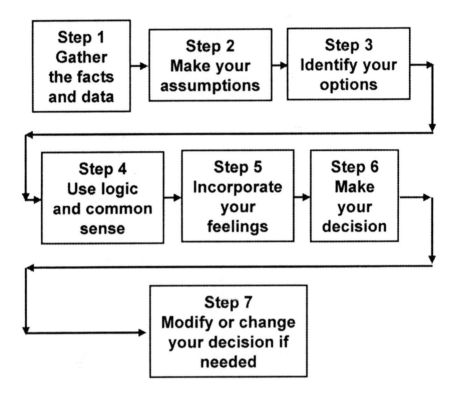

Steps for Effective Decision Making
Figure 7

Step 1: Gather the facts and data

The first step of making an informed decision is to gather facts and data. You have learned this topic in detail in Chapter 5: How to Investigate any Subject.

Step 2: Make your assumptions

The assumptions used while making a decision are important. Per the earlier discussion, ask the following questions about your assumptions:

- Are your assumptions valid?

- If so, why?
- If not, why not?

Step 3: Identify your Options

Once you have identified the options that are available, move to the next step. You have learned this topic in detail in Chapter 8: Fun with Comparison Studies.

Step 4: Use logic and common sense

Combine your logic and common sense with the facts and data, assumptions, knowledge and experience. Ask yourself questions like:

- Does this decision make sense?
- If so, why?
- If not, why not?

Address any risks. Ask questions like:

- Are there any risks involved?
- If so, what are they?
- What can be done to minimize or eliminate these risks?

The amount of time and energy invested in making a decision should be in proportion to the importance of the decision. For example, the time and energy invested in buying a house should be proportionately larger than the amount of time and energy invested in selecting an appliance—or even a car.

Back to Jack

Consider Jack's (who did a trade study on buying a car earlier) motivation for purchasing a car and see if his logic holds up. Here is his thought process:

Jack makes a good salary. He assumes he needs a car because his current car is seven years old and has over 110,000 miles on it. Jack needs reliable transportation for his job. His car has already broken down twice in the last three months.

Jack had a responsible position. If his car broke down at inopportune times he might have missed some important schedules and his company could lose money. This would not reflect well on Jack. Here is Jack's stream of logic:

Stream of Logic	Identified
• My car is older and has 100,000+ miles on it	Fact/Data
• My car has broken down twice in the last 3 months	Fact/Data
• I have a responsible position at work	Fact/Perception
• Missing schedules because of a broken down car could cause my company to lose money	Perception
• My reputation could be damaged if my car continues to break down	Perception
• I make a good salary and can afford a newer car	Fact/Perception
• I need to buy a newer more reliable car	*Decision (Conclusion)*

Jack's Stream of Logic
Figure 8

Jack's conclusion of needing a newer car is backed up by sound logic, common sense and thinking through the task.

Step 5: Incorporate your feelings

Many people use their feelings and emotions to make most, if not all of their decisions. They ask themselves questions such as: Do I like to color, shape, texture and/or feel of this product? Utilizing feelings without backing them up with facts, data and logic can lead to flawed decision making.

Feelings are an important part of any decision. However, they need to be backed up by knowledge, logic and common sense.

The left brain, right brain crossover

The left hemisphere of the brain is used for logical, analytical, rational, and objective reasoning. The right hemisphere is used for intuitive, subjective and holistic thinking. Using only one side of the brain is denying oneself of the full power of the decision making process.

Most people are fully capable of using both parts of their brains to make sound, rational and logical decisions that they feel good about. The *left brain, right brain crossover* is worth developing.

The Left Brain, Right Brain Crossover

People who use only use their left brain and work with facts, data and logic without feelings to make decisions are missing the richness of using their emotions. These individuals deny their feelings because they believe that facts, data, and logic always produce better decisions than feelings and emotions.

Feelings are an integral part of the human condition. Accepting and embracing them during decision making ensures that you will feel good about your decision—now, and later.

On the flip side, those who only "feel" their answers miss the importance of backing up those feelings with information and common sense. Learning the facts and data frequently saves a great deal of money, time, and heartache.

It can be scary to learn the facts and data for someone accustomed to basing decisions on feelings. However, moving out of one's comfort zone and using the left side of the brain ensures balanced and sound decisions.

There are many amazing people who have accomplished much with a strong left brain, right brain crossover. For example, Alan Bean was a Navy test pilot, the Lunar module pilot on Apollo 12 and the forth man to walk on the moon. These jobs required strong left brain thinking using logical, analytical, rational, and objective reasoning.

After resigning from NASA Alan Bean became a full time artist. He paints Apollo's human adventure that is both visionary and historic. Art requires strong right brain thinking using intuitive, subjective and holistic thinking.[1]

Florence Nightingale is another example of a person with an excellent left brain right brain crossover. Many of the nurturing qualities of a good nurse are right brain traits. Her work as a statistician to show the importance of sanitary conditions in healing the sick and wounded used her left brain powers.[2]

"Think left and think right and think low and think high. Oh, the thinks you can think up if you only try!"

—Theodor Geisel (Dr. Suess)

Step 6: Make your decision

Two primary types of decisions are:

1. **A yes or no decision.** For example, should you buy or continue to rent. Another example is: Should you change your career?

2. **Selecting from options available.** Which options should be selected? For example, Jack had options to select when he was choosing a car.

Once you have gathered the facts and data, made good assumptions, used logic and common sense, and incorporated your feelings you are ready to make a decision.

However, before the decision can be made, uncertainty needs to be recognized and addressed.

Most decisions won't be perfect. The facts and data gathered may be lacking, or in conflict. Feelings may waver on a decision. There will be uncertainty to deal with.

Many people are conditioned from an early age to believe that being wrong is bad. This conditioning can hold them back from making decisions when uncertainty is involved—and it is almost always involved. The more complex the decision, the more doubt will be encountered.

Because of the uncertainty encountered, it is natural to be reluctant to make a decision. Here are two reasons to make a decision after you have completed all of the appropriate steps even if aspects of the project, objective or problem are ambiguous. They are:

1. **If you don't make a decision, (in many cases) it will be made for you.** Being a good critical thinker means taking the responsibility and the initiative to make one's own decisions.

2. **Most decisions can be changed or modified—if not immediately, in time.**

Step 7: Modify or change your decision if needed

Frequently, new facts and data become available after you have made a decision. Sometimes this information is relatively insignificant. Other times it is important.

If the new information would have changed your mind if received earlier, then you have two possibilities:

1. **Modify or change your decision (if possible).**

2. **If your decision is difficult (or impossible) to change then determine a way to handle it.** Change it in the future if possible. The application of almost all decisions can be changed in time.

More Decision Making Methods

The Pareto Diagram

(For comparison studies)

Earlier in this book we discussed the 80/20 rule discovered by Vilfredo Pareto. It is illustrated graphically using Pareto's Diagram.

Parato's Diagram is a bar chart that prioritizes information. It shows the relative importance of things by charting them from left to right. It frequently becomes clear that eighty percent of effects are within twenty percent of the components measured.

Here is an example to show how the Pareto Diagram works.

We all use power in our homes or apartments. To save money on this electricity it makes sense to focus efforts on reducing the highest energy users. This can be done by creating a Pareto Diagram of energy costs and usage.

Appliance Cost/Year

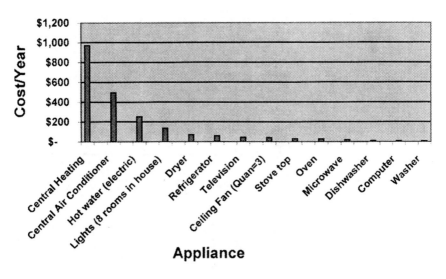

A Pareto Diagram of Appliance Electric Costs
Figure 9

The following section explains how this chart was generated.

Consider fourteen of the top consumers of electricity in a standard home that is 2,100 ft² with 8 rooms. The power consumers are:

- Central heating
- Central air conditioner
- Hot water
- Lights (8 rooms)
- Dryer
- Refrigerator
- Television
- Ceiling fans (3)
- Stove top

- Oven
- Microwave
- Dishwasher
- Computer
- Washer

Home Appliances

Following is a breakdown of typical power consumption and cost. This chart shows appliances in order of highest cost and KW electricity usage.[3]

Electricity Costs		
Appliance	Avg Cost/Year	KW hours/Year
Central Heating	$ 968	11666
Central Air Conditioner	$ 496	5707
Hot water (electric)	$ 251	2889
Lights (8 rooms in house)	$ 135	1551
Dryer	$ 68	786
Refrigerator	$ 60	694
Television	$ 42	482
Ceiling Fan (Quan=3)	$ 40	478
Stove top	$ 28	317
Oven	$ 27	310
Microwave	$ 19	214
Dishwasher	$ 11	128
Computer	$ 10	110
Washer	$ 8	98
Yearly	$ 2,163	25430

Appliance Costs and Power Usage
Table 3

The following Pareto Diagram graphically shows these costs.

Appliance Cost/Year

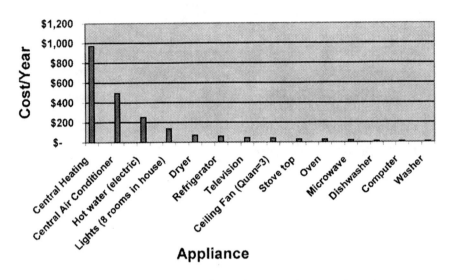

A Pareto Diagram of Appliance Electric Costs
(Figure 9 Repeated)

This is a good example of the 80/20 rule. Heating, air conditioning and hot water are the biggest users of electricity. They cost $1, 715 yearly out of a total electricity cost of $2,163. That's close to 80% of the cost for three out of the fourteen appliances addressed.

To conserve electricity and save money, efforts needs to focus on raising the thermostat temperature in the summer months by a few degrees (to conserve air conditioning) and lowering it by a few degrees in the winter months (to conserve heating). Taking a few less hot showers each month will also save electricity.

The Pareto Diagram shows that lights are the next biggest users; however each individual light is a small part of the electric consumption.

There are positive side effects to focusing on a problem. Addressing the important effects often leads to addressing the lesser important ones as well.

The domino effect–Components are interrelated in decision making. When the important elements are addressed, many of the lesser elements are addressed as a natural side effects. This is known as the *domino effect*.

For example, by consciously adjusting the thermostat a few degrees to conserve energy, and taking less hot showers leads to turning off the lights, computer and television when they aren't being used. Many times this occurs without thinking. Conservation thoughts lead to more conservation thoughts. Your electric bill is lowered further.

The Domino Effect

The Ben Franklin Balance Sheet Close
(For yes or no decisions)

The Ben Franklin balance sheet close is a method used by some top sales people to help clients make a decision. Tom Hopkins a famous sales trainer calls it: "One of the most magnificent closes that have ever come into the selling profession."

Known for his common sense, Ben Franklin originally developed the balance sheet close. He made thousands of wise decisions and used this method to make many of those decisions. It is used to make yes or no decisions.

To use the Ben Franklin close take a clean sheet of paper and draw a vertical line down the center. Next, draw a horizontal line across the paper—near the top. Above the horizontal line and on the left side of the vertical line write the word: "Yes." Underneath it write all the arguments for the decision. On the right side and above the horizontal line write the word: "No." Underneath it write all the arguments against the decision.

When completed, count the number of arguments for the decision on the left side of the paper. Then count the number of arguments against the decision on the right side of the paper. Frequently, the decision becomes obvious.[4]

Earlier we used a stream of logic to determine if Jack should purchase a newer car. Now, the Ben Franklin close will be used for the same example to show how it works.

The "Yes" column is for reasons to buy a car. The "No" column is for reasons against buying a car.

Yes	No
◆ My car is 7 years old ◆ My car has 100,000+ miles on it ◆ My car has broken down twice in 3 months ◆ A nice car would give me better status ◆ I would have fewer worries about being absent from work ◆ I can afford a newer car ◆ I need to buy a newer more reliable car ◆ I have earned it ◆ It would be fun to have a newer car	◆ I currently have no car payments

The Ben Franklin Balance Close Sheet
Figure 10

Jack's decision is straight forward. There are nine good reasons to buy a newer car and only one reason not to. If Jack did not have as good paying job, or his existing car was newer and more reliable the decision might be more difficult.

This example shows that the Ben Franklin Close comes to the same conclusion as the stream of logic example earlier. Each of these decision making methods can be used on a wide array of decisions. Choose the one that is right for you when making a decision.

Thin Slicing
(For quick decisions)

Sometimes decisions need to be made quickly. All of your knowledge, education, experience, reasoning, intuition, common sense and confidence must come together rapidly.

The journalist Malcolm Gladwell calls quick decision making *thin slicing* in his book: *Blink*. Thin slicing is the ability to focus on a small set of critical variables to make a quick decision rather than consciously considering every possible variable.[5]

Many decisions are time dependent. Weighing the amount of information needed before making a decision, against the time available is a challenge.

Examples of when thin slicing is needed: combat, avoiding a car accident, or anything requiring an immediate decision. Another common name for thin slicing is thinking on your feet.

A classic example of using thin slicing on multiple occasions was during the Apollo space program. Gene Kranz (a flight controller on the Mercury, Gemini and Apollo space programs) writes about the need for quick accurate decisions in his book: *Failure is not an Option*. Endless intensive simulations were run with the controllers, flight crew and others before every launch. Everyone's skills had to be *razor sharp* during the actual missions. Decisions had to be accurate and made in *real time*. There was little, and sometimes no room for error. Lives were at stake. Risk was part of their business.

Thin slicing was needed during the Apollo 13 crisis when an explosion on the command module caused damage threatening the lives of the crew members. Members of mission control used differential diagnosis to determine the root cause of the problem. They had to think through and brainstorm options, alternatives, risks and uncertainties. Then, working closely with the crew, and in a few hours they put together a set of procedures that would normally take weeks.

The Apollo 13 crew was returned safely back to earth. It was one of the finest hours of the Apollo space program. Exceptional knowledge, experience, reasoning, training, intuition, common sense, confidence and quickness were all necessary to make this possible.[6]

Gene Kranz sums up how he gained his skills to be a top flight director when he said:

> "The flight director's ultimate training comes at the console, working real problems, facing the risks, making irrevocable decisions."

Thin slicing is another good reason to hone your critical thinking skills. Although you may not be faced with instant life and death decisions, you will (on occasions) have to make quick decisions. The better your skills and critical thinking are, coupled with training and quickness, the more prepared you will be to make sound decisions in the blink of an eye!

Looking Forward

Many important critical thinking skills have been presented in the first nine chapters of this book. The next step is to learn how to build strong relationships so you can use the rich resources of other people when critically thinking. That is the focus of the next chapter.

Connections

Chapter 10

How to Connect with Others

"The individual is the central, rarest, most precious capital resource of our society"

—Peter F. Drucker

We have discussed the importance of working with others when critically thinking. This requires building solid relationships. To build these relationships, strong communication skills are needed. That is the focus of this chapter.

We Speak Volumes

Peter Drucker is one of the primary business critical thinkers of the twentieth century. Many of his management ideas have worked their way into conventional wisdom. Here is what the Harvard Business review says about him:

"Father of modern management, social commentator, preeminent business philosopher, Peter F. Drucker has been writing about management for sixty years."

Peter Drucker had enormous respect for people. At times he has been known to ask more questions than deliver answers. His feeling on communication is clear.

"The most important thing in communication is to hear what isn't being said."

—Peter Drucker

This insightful statement says a great deal. We communicate in everything we say and do. Our words, body language and facial expressions are the common ways we communicate. Beyond that; the way we walk, dress, our attitude, disposition, and a wide array of other subtle, but powerful signals, communicate who we are and what we are about to others.

People who treat others with respect and dignity have far richer relationships than those who only see others as objects in their way, or as a means to an end.

To improve your communication skill you need strong fundamental principles. The important ones are:

Key Principles of Good Communication

Principle # 1: Our uniqueness affects how we communicate with others.

Principle #2: Being a student of people significantly increases the ability to communicate and connect with others.

Principle #3: Effective listening is an integral part of good communication.

Principle #4: Credibility coupled with sincerity, honesty and respect are the cornerstones of a fine reputation.

Principle # 5: It is important to carefully choose words and phrases when using remote forms of communication.

Principle #6: Helping others feel important will result in great service.

Principle #7: Conflicts are best managed by focusing on the issues rather than the individual.

Connections

It is beyond the scope of this book to go into detail on applying these principals of communication. However, since good communication skills are important for critical thinking when working with others I have created a book that teaches these skills. It is called: *CONNECTIONS.*[1]

If you feel powerful Connections would be helpful in your quest for better critical thinking skills (or communication in general) it can be obtained from my website. Please see the front cover of this book for my website location.

Looking Forward

You have built up powerful critical thinking concepts, methods, and resources to make informed decisions, complete projects and achieve objectives. The next step is to use what you have learned to look forward. The next section is all about designing an exciting future for yourself.

In the next chapter you will learn about your multiple intelligences and how they can be used to improve your life. You will also learn about the power of convergent and divergent thinking skills and how they can be improved.

Your Future!

Chapter 11

Discovering Your Multiple Intelligences

"The world is full of magical things patiently waiting
for our wits to grow sharper"

—Bertrand Russell

We are each unique with strengths and weaknesses that are different than those of anyone else. Your primary question is:

How can I apply my natural and developed talents to make the most productive, interesting and enjoyable life for myself?

This section teaches you about your uniqueness and your many intelligences and how to put them to use. You will learn about convergent and divergent thinking skills and how they relate to intelligence.

123

Our Multiple Intelligences

Significant work has explained the various types of human intelligences. Research published argues that the usual view of human intelligence is far too narrow. Standard IQ testing only tests Logical-Mathematical Intelligence and Linguistic Intelligence. These tests don't help predict success or happiness in life. Nor do they test the other intelligences. Let's discuss these other intelligences in more detail.

Daniel Goleman teaches *Emotional Intelligence* in his book by that name. He argues convincingly that Emotional Intelligence is a essential factor in determining personal and professional success. Goleman explains that individuals who are able to tap into self-awareness, self-discipline and empathy are usually happier, healthier and more successful personally and professionally.[1]

Before Daniel Goleman's book, Howard Gardner did pioneering work on the theory of Multiple Intelligences in the early 1980's. Although the concept of Multiple Intelligences had existed for some time, Gardner brought fresh thoughts to the subject. His book *"Frames of Mind"* explains a non exhaustive list of human intelligences. Thomas Armstrong helped interpret these intelligences for the general population in his book: *7 Kinds of Smart.* [2, 3] They are:

- **Logical-Mathematical Intelligence**—People who have this intelligence can apply it to do mathematical problems of varying complexity. It is also pattern recognition ability and applying a stream of logic to get answers to questions. It is a primary component of convergent thinking skills. It is first of the two intelligences that western academics evaluate using the usual IQ tests.

- **Linguistic Intelligence**—This enables an individual to develop the ability to understand language, word speech, and the methods used for these. It is the second intelligence that western academics are evaluated with using the usual IQ tests.

- **Music Intelligence**—This enables an individual to have an internal feel and sense for music. Ludwig van Beethoven's had this ability. He wrote beautiful music such as *Ode to Joy*, the 4th movement of his 9th symphony. Individuals who have music intelligence may or may not have a strong understanding of music theory.

- **Bodily-Kinesthetic Intelligence**—This enables an individual to excel as an athlete such as sports player, dancer or gymnast. Eye hand and body coordination are big factors in body kinesthetic intelligence.

- **Spatial-Intelligence**—This intelligence provides the ability to see things spatially. It is an important aspect of an athlete to sense his environment during competition. A gymnast would not do well if he didn't know where the parallel bar was spatially during a flip. This is also a skill that good architects must have in order to see the spatial requirements of a structure that he is designing.

- **Interpersonal Intelligence**—This enables an individual to interact and relate to others effectively. Daniel Goleman's work on Emotional Intelligence explains this intelligence in depth.

- **Intrapersonal Intelligence**–This is the intelligence of the inner-self. A person who can easily access his or her own feelings and emotional states by being introspective has intrapersonal intelligence. Utilizing this intelligence allows an individual to have an enriched and purposeful life.

Thomas Armstrong in his book; *7 Kinds of Smart*, says:

> "The message is clear: IQ tests have been measuring something that might be more properly called school-house giftedness, while real intelligence takes a much broader range of skills."

Whether there are seven kinds of intelligences or more is not that crucial, nor is the possibility that there are subsets to any or all of these different types of intelligences.

What is important is that if there are multiple intelligences, (and I for one agree), then a whole new world of opportunities awaits those who are willing to learn their true strengths and passions in life.

Formal schooling puts strong emphasis on Logical-Mathematical and Linguistic intelligence. Musical Intelligence (music class), Body Kinesthetic and Spatial-Intelligence (gym), Interpersonal Intelligence (intertwined in all classes—getting along with others), and Intrapersonal Intelligence (not taught much) are considered lower priority intelligences in our schools. Logical-Mathematical and Linguistic intelligences are clearly important. However, knowing about and exploring your other intelligences is beneficial as well.

There are several reasons that people are held back from pursuing their most prominent intelligences in school and in work. However, there are resources to learn about them and how they can be pursued.

1. **Peer, teacher, parent pressures to focus on math, science and linguistics**

   As a critical thinker you have the ability to investigate your own multiple intelligences.

2. **Not knowing what the sources of your true abilities are**

   Testing is available to discover your strengths in the other areas of intelligence. You can do your own investigation to locate testing for multiple intelligences using the critical thinking investigation process discussed earlier in this book.

3. **The path to a successful career based in some of the other intelligences is nowhere near as clear as it is for careers in logic, math, science and linguistics**

   Discovering possible career opportunities taking advantage of other types of intelligences can be found using critical thinking investigation.

4. **Other career pays more**

   It is possible to pursue your other intelligences while working a full-time career.

Knowing that you possess other intelligences and the ability to pursue your natural gifts (full or part time) can be a liberating experience and a spiritual awakening!

Convergent vs. Divergent Thinking

Convergent and divergent thinking skills are both aspects of intelligence and critical thinking.

Convergent Thinking is the bringing facts and data together from various sources and then applying logic and knowledge to solve problems or achieve objectives.

The deductive logic that the fictional character Sherlock Homes used is a good example of convergent thinking. Gathering various tidbits of facts and data he was able to put the pieces of a puzzle together and come up with a logical answer to the question: Who done it?

> "When you have eliminated the impossible, whatever remains, however improbable, must be the truth."
>
> —Sir Arthur Conan Doyle

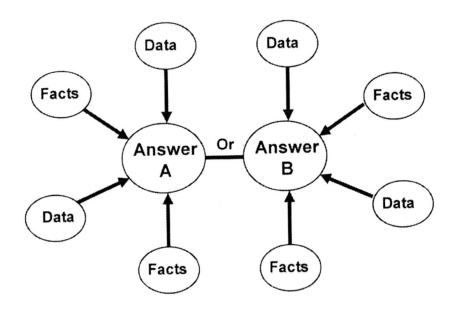

Convergent Thinking
Figure 11

Divergent Thinking is thinking outwards instead of inward. It is the ability to develop original and unique ideas and then come up with a problem solution or achieve an objective.

Einstein was a strong divergent thinker. He asked simple questions and then did mental exercises to solve problems. For example, as a young man Einstein asked himself what it would be like to ride on a beam of light. It took him many years of *thought experiments*, however the answer helped him develop the special theory of relativity. Thought experiments are imagined scenarios to understand the way thing are.

Years later, Einstein improved on this theory to take gravity into effect in his equations and came up with the general theory of relativity. Many physicists today are still stunned by Einstein's ability to come up with his general theory concept using thought experiments.

"Imagination is more important than knowledge."
—Albert Einstein

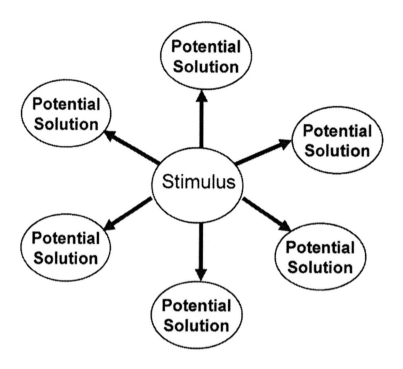

Divergent Thinking
Figure 12

Standard IQ tests gauge convergent thinking. Pattern recognition, testing knowledge, logic thought flow and the ability to solve problems can all be tested and graded.

There are no accurate tests able to measure divergent thinking skills. It's not surprising that creative skills can't be tested.

How would one construct a test to determine divergent thinking capabilities? Did Leonardo da Vinci's creation of the Mona Lisa take more brain power than Einstein's equation $E = MC^2$? Is the design of the Opera house in Sydney Australia more creative than Margaret Mitchell's novel *Gone with the Wind?* Is Alvin Toffler's book *Future Shock* more inspired than Salvador Dali's painting of the melting clocks?

Who's to say which of these examples is more creative? Does public opinion decide what how much creativity was required for something, or is in the eye of the beholder? These are interesting philosophical questions, and ones that are enjoyable to talk about at parties, however aren't useful to discover how to creatively think.

A more useful question is: How can convergent and divergent thinking be improved and utilized to strengthen your critical thinking skills? Convergent and divergent thinking skills are both important to critical thinking. Not only that, they are interrelated.

Deductive reasoning looks inward to find a solution, while divergent reasoning looks outward for a solution. Following the facts and data to determine the answer to a problem is not significantly different than having a spark of a thought and then coming up with a solution. Some of the same mental processes are used. Both require critical thinking skills to be effective. Both are used for solving problems, doing projects and achieving objectives.

In other words, Convergent and Divergent thinking skills are two sides to the same coin—of critical thinking. One without the other doesn't make sense. Both start with asking simple questions from a curious mind. Both can be strengthened by an insatiable curiosity and strong willingness to learn about the world and the people in it. Here is an example.

The dream of traveling beyond the reaches of earth's gravity has been around since men and women first looked up at the stars. It's wasn't until the middle of the 20th century that technology became available that would make space travel possible.

On October 14th of 1957 Sputnik was launched by the Russians and the space race began. The United States was shocked when beaten by the Russians in technology. In response the US formed the National Aeronautics and Space Administration in 1958.

In the early 1960s John Kennedy sent letters to top people in the aerospace industry including Wernher von Braun. He asked how the US could beat the Russians in the space race. Wernher von Braun answered saying that the United States couldn't beat them in building a space station; however we could beat them with a manned flight to the surface of the moon.

John Kennedy had done his homework by getting expert advice before giving his famous speech vowing to transport a man to the moon and bring him safely home by the end of the decade. His speech helped galvanize some 390,000 NASA employees and contractors to work as a cohesive team and accomplish one of the greatest feats of history in less than a decade![4]

Kennedy used facts and data to determine how we could beat the Russians into space. That was primarily convergent thinking. The required development of many new technologies to design and build the rockets, spacesuits, lunar modules and other equipment to perform this amazing feat required a great deal of divergent thinking.

Moon Landing

"The only way to discover the limits of the possible is to go beyond them into the impossible."

—Arthur C. Clarke

The case for divergent skills improvement

Schooling helps to train the mind in problem solving of the convergent type, however it tends to dampen or inhibit divergent thinking skills (with the exception of good teachers—and there are many).

IQ tests frequently have the same effect. They tend to motivate those who do well on convergent thinking skill tests, but un-motivate others who don't do as well.

Howard Gardner states:

> "Intelligence tests rarely assess skill in the assimilating new information or in solving new problems. This bias toward "crystallized" rather than "fluid" knowledge can have some astounding consequences."

He goes on to quote the Soviet psychologist Lev Vygotsky in saying:

> "Intelligence tests fail to yield any indication of an individual's *zone of potential.*"

The case for strengthening divergent thinking skills is strong. The methods that have been discussed in this book will help you improve both your convergent and your divergent critical thinking skills.

Looking Forward

Now you can have an exciting future for yourself. The next (and final) chapter presents the steps to create that future. Enjoy!

Chapter 12

Creating an Exciting Future For Yourself!

"For tomorrow belongs to the people who prepare for it today"

—African Proverb

Which Future?

The Shape of Things to Come!

We are on the edge of an amazing future. What changes lay ahead? What skills will you need to be successful and happy? Will you be ready?

Alvin and Heidi Toffler are futurists. They have studied and written predictions of the future for decades.

Their first book, *Future Shock* was released back in 1970. It was thoroughly researched and critically thought through. Many of their predictions came true.

Their latest book, *Revolutionary Wealth* released in 2006 also makes predictions about the future. Since their past books were proven to be accurate on many topics, it's fair to assume that their latest book will provide many insightful thoughts about the future.

Here are some key excerpts from their work.

The Wealth System

"If the First Wave wealth system was chiefly based on growing things, and the Second Wave on making things, the Third Wave wealth system is increasingly based on serving, *thinking, knowing and experiencing* … The new wealth system demands a complete shake-up in the way *increasingly temporary skill sets* are organized for increasingly temporary purposes throughout the economy. Nothing is more deeply fundamental to the creation of wealth."

Knowledge

"In each of us there is a crowded, invisible warehouse full of *knowledge* and its precursor *data and information*. But unlike a warehouse, it is also a workshop in which we—or, more accurately, the electrochemicals in our brains—continually shift, add, subtract, combine and rearrange numbers, symbols, words, images, and memories, combining them with emotions to form *new thoughts*."

Cross Disciplinary Knowledge Required

"More and more jobs require *cross-disciplinary knowledge*, so that we find increasing need for hyphenated backgrounds—"Astro-biologist," "bio-physicist," "environmental-engineer," "forensic-accountant.""

A New Dawn

"Living at the dawn of this century, we are direct or indirect participants in the *design of a new civilization* with a revolutionary wealth system at its core. Will this process complete itself—or will the still incomplete wealth revolution come to a crashing halt?" [1]

The message is clear. Those who will succeed and prosper in the coming years will have the following skills and backgrounds:

- Decision making
- Knowledge
- Schooling
- Experience
- Reasoning
- Intuition
- Common sense
- Confidence

These skills and background can be boiled down to three words: Critical Thinking Skills. With these skills you will be prepared for whatever challenges the future presents.

Are You Ready for the Coming Changes?

Today changes are happening at an increasing rate in the world and in our personal lives. With more choices than ever before we are constantly bombarded with opportunities to change and grow. It can be dizzying at times.

Whether you are sixteen, sixty or any other age, the need to grow, adjust and adapt are crucial to being happy and prosperous. You may be trying to decide on your first career, or your fourth one. Or, you may be preparing for retirement. Even if you are satisfied with your work, you may want to consider new interesting and fun activities or hobbies for your spare time.

On the other hand, you may currently be happy with these areas of your life. Your career is going well, and you enjoy your outside activities.

Either way, changes in one or more of these areas is inevitable—if not now, later. Security in life is frequently an illusion—and today this is true more than ever. Helen Keller had an amazing life despite the fact that she was blind and deaf. One of her famous quotes is:

> "Life is either a daring adventure or nothing. Security does not exist in nature, nor do the children of men as a whole experience it. Avoiding danger is no safer in the long run than exposure."

Using Inflection Points to Improve Your Future

One of the primary components of critical thinking is asking tough questions. And, critical thinking can be used to look inward or outward.

In previous chapters questions were asked when defining and completing projects, achieve objectives and solving problems. Those were *external questions*. *This* chapter will show you what questions to ask to improve your life. These are *internal questions*.

To answer these questions you will use many of the same critical thinking methods and concepts discussed earlier. You will be introduced to some new methods and concepts.

Why do you change what you do in life? In other words, what can cause you to venture out from your comfort zone and consider a new career, outside activity or venture?

The answer is that most major changes in life are cause by events called *inflection points*. An inflection point is an event that changes how you view the world, who you are, or your life in general.

Think 9-11. People in the United States felt safer before that day. After 9-11 we realized our vulnerability to terrorists. There are many inflection points in our history. For example:

In early 1776 Thomas Paine published a 46 page pamphlet called *Common Sense.* It helped inspire the writing of the Declaration of Independence and motivated a nation.

The book was written for the common man and was estimated to have sold 120,000 copies within three months of publication and 500,000 copies within a year. It is worth noting that this was in the United States when there were only 3 million people—and many couldn't read!

John Adams and others had been arguing for the United States to become an independent nation. The release of Paine's *Common Sense* was the inflection point that caused the nation to become independent.

Thomas Paine knew that the time was right to inspire the people to take action. He argued convincingly that the young nation had to make a choice for independence now—not later. Paine explained that within fifty years the personal interests of individuals who would acquire status and money by then would resist such a change. And, the colonies would be more established and would resist such a change. [2, 3]

> "A long habit of not thinking a thing wrong gives it a superficial appearance of being right."
>
> —Thomas Paine

Change in life is usually gradual. But, inflection points have great power to change you. Most inflection points will start with a single decision.

Years ago I made a decision to get a Masters of Business at Pepperdine University in California. It was an inflection point that changed my life positively in many ways.

I studied longer and harder when I worked for my master's degree than any other time in my formal education. I took on the challenge because I had ownership in my education. It validated the thought that we are more motivated when we have a vested interest in what we want to accomplish. It all started with a decision to further my education and marketability.

Most positive inflection points that occur in people's lives that start with a decision; examples are:

- Deciding to stay in high school and graduate
- Deciding to go to college
- Deciding to buy a home
- Deciding to be committed to being financially secure
  - By not allowing excessive dept
  - By studying and investing wisely
- Deciding to start a business
- Deciding to continually grow as a person
- Deciding to be a good critical thinker

Everyday you make other less impacting decisions. However, they all have consequences. Each decision you make, each path you take, each risk you take helps to define who you are and who you will become. Investing the time to think through, investigate, weigh options, and then choosing your decisions carefully creates a better life.

"Either do or do not; there is no try."

—George Lucas

Passion and Time Urgency

"Success is not the key to happiness. Happiness is the key to success. If you love what you are doing, you'll be a success."

—Albert Schweitzer

Having passion for what you do is important. It is what gets you up in the morning. It is what you need to feel useful. It is what powers you. And, it is related to time.

Time can be a friend or an enemy. The unmotivated person has the same amount of time each week as the CEO of a major corporation. However, what each of these individuals does with his time is profoundly different.

Time is an enemy if a person constantly procrastinates, if he fears leaving his comfort zone, and if he doesn't pursue his passion. Time will pass and he will be no closer to achieving that which he wants out of life.

Time is a friend if you pursue your passion. It feels great to have a purpose and to pursue it.

As famous sales trainer Tom Hopkins has said:

> "I must do the most productive thing possible at every given moment."

He explained that sometimes that statement means working hard; sometimes it means resting when needed, and sometimes it means investing time with others. However it is always means moving forward towards what you want out of life.

> "Lost time is never found again"
>
> —Benjamin Franklin

To begin the process of discovering your passions, ask yourself the following questions:

- Where do I want "to be" in a week?
- Where do I want "to be" in a month?
- Where do I want "to be" in a year?
- Where do I want "to be" in five years?
- Where do I want "to be" in ten years?

"To be" can require many things. It can require starting a new dance class next week, or moving to a nicer place next month. It can require going back to school in a year for a degree to improve your status and salary. It can necessitate changing careers in five years to enjoy more interesting life work.

Each decision has implications. A decision to move in a month or two means the planning and packing must start soon. Changing to a new career in one to five years may require going back to school to get a degree in a new field.

When you decide what you want to accomplish, big or small, it helps put urgency to your decision and makes it real. Without any time urgency many dreams go unfulfilled. That's human nature.

Make a Life List and Check it Twice

Listing what you want to accomplish in your life is useful and recommended. It can be done at an early age; or at any age.

John Goddard who is a famous adventurer and motivational speaker decided early in his life to make a list of goals he wanted to accomplish. That list became the inflection point that guided him through the years.

At the age of 15 John Goddard wrote down the 127 goals he wanted to reach in his lifetime. The categories were wide and deep. Here are just a few of his goals.

- **Explore:** The Nile, Amazon & Congo
- **Climb:** Mt Kilimanjaro, Mt Rainier & Mt Fuji
- **Swim in:** Lake Victoria, Lake Titicaca & Lake Superior
- **Photograph:** Iguaçu Falls in Brazil & Victoria Falls in Rhodesia
- **Study Primitive Cultures in:** The Congo, Brazil, Borneo & Australia

- **Explore Underwater:** The Coral reefs of Florida & the Great Barrier Reef
- **Visit:** The Great Wall of China, the Panama and Suez canals & the Taj Mahal
- **Accomplish:** Becoming an Eagle Scout, diving in a submarine & learning to fence

Six decades later he has accomplished well over 100 of his goals. It all started with a list of decisions!

In the 1980s I read about John Goddard in a readers digest article. I was impressed with his will and accomplishments. I hoped then that one day I might meet him.

A few years later I had the great pleasure to meet and dine with John Goddard at his home. It was quite an experience.

Before dinner John showed me around his home and took me into a room with artifacts from around the world. He gently joked with me and the mood was light. He walked me over to where there was a primitive sword hung on the wall. John reached over and pulled the sword half-way out of its sheath, and said to me in a serious tone: "This sword must draw blood if it is ever pulled out of its sheath!" Then, he slowly put the sword back.

His message was clear. Just as a sword isn't taken out unless it is used; we need to finish what we start to be successful in life. It was a fitting lesson for everyone who wants to improve their life.

John Goddard's zest for life and adventure has inspired many people. When a writer asked about John's age he responded:

> "In our family we don't keep track of years; we keep track of experience. Age is only important in terms of wine and cheese!"

Whether you are eight or eighty, having a list helps you plan for an interesting future full of purpose and enjoyment.

Visioning Your Own Future

What are your goals in life? Have you thought about them lately? When your life is over, will they be fulfilled or not?

These can be tough questions. They require an honest look at your successes, failures, opportunities taken and opportunities lost. These questions need to be asked to decide on a purposeful future. A useful method to do this is to use *self-reflection*. Self-reflection is taking an honest look at your strengths, weaknesses and what you want out of life.

A good way to minimize the sting of self-reflection is to be as unemotional and as objective about yourself as possible. Imagine you are looking at a close friend's life (it helps to be a close friend to yourself) and making recommendations for a happier life. This requires you to not judge yourself of past failures, opportunities missed or shortcomings. Focus objectively on what you can do to improve your life.

If you are uncomfortable with a written list, make a mental list. However, a written list of what you want to do during your lifetime has a sobering effect. It forces you to look deep inside and decide what you really want. Your list can be a few items, or many. And, it can be changed throughout time as needed.

This list will be your inflection point. It will help you crystallize the decision to pursue those things in your life that are important to you.

To discover what you want to do, define some life goals by working backwards to determine what you want to do in the future. This is done by doing some *blue sky thinking* using the *rocking chair test.*

Blue sky thinking is sitting in a comfortable chair, getting a cup of coffee or warm tea, kicking back your feet and contemplating a deep subject.

The rocking chair test is a simple mental exercise imagining that you are in a rocking chair in the final years of your life. These questions use your personal history as a guide to help you decide on potential improvements for your future. To perform the rocking chair test, ask yourself the following questions:

- Did I choose the career (or careers) that I enjoyed?
  - If so, why?
  - If not, why not?
- What accomplishments did I achieve?
- What accomplishments that I wanted did I not achieve?
  - What held me back?
- Which activities did I do that I wanted to?
  - What encouraged me to do them?
- Which activities didn't I do that I would have liked to?
  - What held me back?
- If I had my life to do over again what would I do differently?
- What would I have kept the same?
- What things did I choose to do in my life that made me happy?
  - Why?
- Could I have done more of them?
  - Why didn't I?

Thinking through the answers to the rocking chair test questions will form the basis of a more successful, happy and useful life. That's an easy statement to make, but has significant challenges.

Everyone would like to *cherry pick* their lives. Cherry picking is to only do those things that most interest us.

Responsibilities, obligations, challenges, fear of failure and being afraid to step out of comfort zones hold people back from doing everything they want to do in life. Although people can't do everything, most lives are long enough to do much of what is desired.

For example, Grandma Moses a famous artist who enjoyed drawing as a child didn't start painting as a career until she was in her seventies.

She had spent most of her adult life as a farmer's wife and the mother of five children.

> "Life is what you make it, always has been, always will be."
>
> —Grandma Moses

Once in a great while an individual needs a radical change in his or her life. Here is an example of a person who felt that need and changed his reputation.

Alfred Noble is best known for creating the Noble Peace Prizes. He was also an inventor who had hundreds of patents including the invention of dynamite.

Noble had invented dynamite to improve mining activities. He was distraught when it was used for killing and destruction in war.

Alfred Noble's was inspired to create the Noble Peace Prizes when he read a premature obituary of himself, published in error by a French newspaper that mistook Alfred for Ludvig his brother who had just died. The article condemned Alfred as *The merchant of death!*

The article disturbed Noble. It was an inflection point that motivated him to critically think of a way to be more positively remembered.

Alfred Noble was able to change how he would be remembered. He decided to leave most of his worth, after dying, to the establishment of six prizes. These were for physics, chemistry, physiology or medicine, literature, peace and economics. They were for "those who, during the previous year, shall have conferred the greatest benefit to mankind." These awards are known today as the highly sought after Noble Peace Prizes.[4]

> "Reputation is what men and women think of us; character is what God and angels know of us."
>
> —Thomas Paine

Finding Alternative Careers and Activities

Deciding on a career is personal. It is based on interests, financial need, obligations, responsibilities, motivation, and more. The methods and techniques taught in this book will help you to learn about and to make decisions on choices that you have investigated and have an interest in.

To assist you in investigating potential alternative career opportunities, outside activities, your multiple intelligences, and the future, here are some books worth looking into.

- *What Color is your Parachute—A Practical Manual for Job-Hunters and Career-Changers*
  By Richard Nelson Bolles

- *I Could Do Anything If I Only Knew* What It Was—*How to Discover What You Really Want and How to Get It*
  By Barbara Sher with Barbara Smith

- *Do What You Are—Discover the Perfect Career for You Through the Secrets of Personality Type—Revised and Updated Edition Featuring E-careers for the 21st Century*
  By Paul D. Tieger and Barbara Barron-Tieger

- *Wishcraft—How to Get What You Really Want*
  By Barbara Sher with Annie Gottlieb

- 7 Kinds of Smart—*Identifying and Developing Your Multiple Intelligences*
  By Thomas Armstrong

- *Revolutionary Wealth—How it will be created and how it will change our lives.*
  By Alvin and Heidi Toffler

Your Journey Continues!

Through these pages we have taken a journey together. My purpose has been to guide you to create a critical thinking mindset. My wish is that you continue to strengthen your critical thinking skills by increasing your curiosity about the world.

Ask questions, listen to, and think through the answers. These simple habits will improve your critical thinking skills. Like any ability, critical thinking skills will improve with practice. In the words of Carl Sagan who helped expand the universe for millions by teaching about it:

> "Ask courageous questions. Do not be satisfied with superficial answers. Be open to wonder and at the same time subject all claims to knowledge, without exception, to intense skeptical scrutiny. Be aware of human fallibility. Cherish your species and your planet. "[5]

We have come to the end of this book, but not critical thinking. To assist you with application of what this book has taught please refer to the following sections:

- References and Notes
- Appendix A: Critical Thinking Vocabulary
- Appendix B: Your Guide to Critical Thinking Concepts
- Appendix C: Figures and Tables
- Appendix D: Vacation Planning Forms
- Appendix E: Comparison Study Forms
- Appendix F: Illustrations

Feel free to contact me with your questions and comments. You can locate me through my website which has interesting and fun information, resources, methods and articles on critical thinking.

www.chuckclayton.com

And finally:

I wish you great success and happiness in discovering
The Lost Art of Critical Thinking!

Chuck Clayton

08/01/07

References
and
Appendixes

References and Notes

Introduction

1   From the American Institute for Research "New study of college students finds some are graduating with only basic skills". January 19, 2006.

Chapter 1
Key Elements of Critical Thinking

1   *Florence Nightingale*, www.Wikipedia.org from Feb 2, 2007.

2   Nancy Gondo, *One Man's Ascent to Greatness—Focus helped Sir Edmund Hillary climb to the top of the world* Investors Business Daily, June 12, 2003, p.A4.

3   Christopher L. Tyner, *Milton Friedman's Free Mind Favors Free Markets* Investors Business Daily, March 2, 2006.

4   O'Neil, William J. *How to Make Money in Stocks—A Winning System in Good Times or Bad* (New York, NY, McGraw-Hill)

Chapter 2
Land Mines to Critical Thinking!

1   *Indian Removal Act of 1830, and Trail of Tears*, www.Wikipedia.org from Feb 2, 2007.

Chapter 4
How to Solve Mysteries!

1   Cringely, Robert X. *Accidental Empires—How the Boys of Silicon Valley Make Their Millions, Battle Foreign Competition, and Still Can't Get A Date* (HarperCollins Publishers, Inc. New York, NY 1992,1996)

2   Marie Curie and Jane Goodall, LHJ *100 Most Important Women of the Century 1999*

3   Rigg, Alan. *How to Beat the 80/20 Rule in Selling—Why Most Salespeople Don't Perform and What to Do About It* (Tucson AZ: Hats off Books 2003, 2004).

4   Toffler, Alvin and Heidi. *Revolutionary Wealth—How it will be created and how it will change our lives.* (Toronto: Random House of Canada Limited 2006).

5   Gladwell, Malcomb. *The Tipping Point—How Little Things Can Make a Big Difference* (Boston, New York, London: Little, Brown and Company, 2000).

6   Curt Schleier, *President George Washington Founding Father: His sense of duty, honor set the standard for the nation.* Investors Business Daily, February 21, 2006.

Chapter 5
How to Investigate any Subject

1   Internet searches can start from using a search engine or going directly to a virtual bookstore. This is a personal decision of which to search first.

2   Fresener, Scott & Pat. *How to Print T-Shirts … for Fun and Profit!* (Tempe AZ, Southwest Screen Print ind., Inc. 1980).

Chapter 9
How to Make Wise Decisions

[1] Bean, Alan, with Andrew Chaikin. *Apollo—An Eyewitness Account by Astronaut/Explores Artist/Moonwalker Alan Bean* (Greenwich Workshop Press Inc. Shelton, Connecticut 1998).

[2] *Florence Nightingale,* www.Wikipedia.org from Feb 2, 2007.

[3] The information for electrical usage is from the Tucson Electric Power Company. Your home power will vary due to usage, current rates, house size, and where you live.

[4] Hopkins, Tom. *How to Master the Art of Selling* (Warner Books Edition, Champion Press, Scottsdale Arizona 1982).

[5] Gladwell, Malcolm. *Blink—The Power of Thinking Without Thinking* (Little Brown and Company, New York, NY, 2005).

[6] Kranz, Gene. *Failure is not an Option—Mission Control from Mercury to Apollo 13 and Beyond* (Simon and Schuster, New York, NY, 2000).

Chapter 10
Connections

[1] Clayton, Charles Walker. *Connections—Change your Paradigm, Change Your Life 2nd edition (Ide House, Radcliffe,2005)*

Chapter 11
Exploring Your Multiple Intelligences

[1] Goleman, Daniel. *Emotional Intelligence—Why it can matter more than IQ* (Bantam Books, New York, NY, 1994).

[2] Gardner, Howard. *Frames of Mind—The Theory of Multiple Intelligences* (Basic Books New York, NY, 1993).

[3] Armstrong, Thomas. *7 Kinds of Smart—Identifying and Developing Your Much Intelligences* (Penguin Books, New York, NY, 1993).

4   Buckbee, Ed with Schirra Wally, *The Real Space Cowboys* (Apogee Books, Burlington, Ontario Canada, 2005)

Chapter 12
Creating an Exciting Future for Yourself!

1   Toffler, Alvin and Heidi. *Revolutionary Wealth—How it will be created and how it will change our lives* (Toronto: Random House of Canada Limited 2006).

2   Jed Graham, *Founding Father Thomas Paine* Investors Business Daily, June 7, 2006, p.A4.

3   Paine, Thomas. *Common Sense* (New York, Barnes and Noble Books 1995)

4   Alfred Noble, www.Wikipedia.org from Jan 19, 2007.

5   Michael Mink, *Billions and Billions of Stars-Visionary Carl Sagan's passion, drive helped expand the universe for millions* Investors Business Daily, December 12, 2006.

Appendix A

Critical Thinking Vocabulary

The following is a list of key words and phrases that are part of the critical thinking language. The definitions of the words and phrases are provided here as well as in the chapter they are first described in.

Chapter 1
Key Elements of Critical Thinking

Thinking through: Reviewing alternatives, options, risks, uncertainties and final goal helps ensure informed decisions and taking appropriate actions.

Stream of logic: A logical progression of thoughts that can lead to a rational solution when doing a project or achieving an objective. It can also be used when solving a problem or answering a question. A stream of logic is also known as a train of thought.

Learning the ropes: A term commonly used that means non-intuitive learning.

Frame of reference: Experience, education, upbringing, culture and a wide array of other factors contribute to how someone views the world.

Face value: Not questioning whether something is correct or incorrect.

Comfort Zone: Things that you feel comfortable with.

Climbing out of one's box: Leaving one's comfort zone.

Chapter 2
Land Mines to Critical Thinking!

Land mines in critical thinking: Threats to the critical thinking process.

Sanity check: Asking whether your thinking is logical and rational.

Sounding board: A friend or colleague who will let you know if you are thinking logically and rationally about a subject.

Norm of thinking: What is reflected by radio, television, news papers, magazines and the Internet.

Chapter 3
What are some Critical Questions?

Red flag: A bad feeling.

Digging deeper: Not taking things at face value and doing more investigation.

Laugh test: When the information is so ridiculous that you know it has to be wrong.

Second opinion: Asking a trusted colleague or friend about his or her interpretation of information.

Chapter 4
How to Solve Mysteries!

The 80/20 rule: A rough order of magnitude on how the world operates. It governs many scenarios in life in which 80 percent of the results come from 20 percent of the inputs.

Trial and error: Trying something to see if it works. If it doesn't work, try something else.

Root cause—The primary cause of a problem.

Differential Diagnosis: A form of scientific reasoning commonly used by doctors in the medical profession to diagnose a medical condition. It is used in other field as well.

Transference: When a method of critical thinking can be used in another field.

Tipping point: Is the point at which ideas, or messages, or behaviors of a population changes rapidly. It is caused by contagious behavior.

Contagious behavior: Similar to an epidemic, the behavior of the general population is changed because of the behavior of a small percentage of people.

Broken Windows theory: If small quality of life crimes such as broken windows are allowed then people will assume no one cares and no one is in charge. Lawlessness will increase.

Act as if: A behavior that encourages respect from others.

Reinventing the wheel: Solving a problem using an new idea instead of using a solution that has already proved to work.

Chapter 5
How to Investigate any Subject

Data mining: The process of locating useful information when investigating.

Just in time learning: Effective data mining that invests your time to learn what you need to know, when you need to know it.

Information overload: When you feel buried in information and have difficulty knowing what to do next.

Blind alleys: A path of investigation that takes you in a direction that won't lead to the information you are looking for.

Wrapped around the axle: Looking at the same information again and again expecting it to yield something useful when it has little that you need.

Algorithm: A procedure used for solving a problem.

Interpreter: A person who can explain difficult subject matter by restating it for people who want to learn about it, but aren't in that particular field.

The Point of Diminishing Returns: The point during investigation when your time and energy generate minimal worthwhile facts and data. It can be though of as the opposite of the 80/20 rule. It is determined by a personal decision based on knowledge, experience, reasoning, intuition and common sense.

Chapter 6
How to Do Projects and Achieve Objectives

Begging the question: When one question leads to another question or series of questions.

Framing: Defining what you need to do a project or objective.

Check list: A list of questions that need to be answered in order to do a project, complete an objective or solve a problem.

Lessons learned: Is determining what went right, what went wrong and what could have been done differently after completing a project, achieving an objective, or solving a problem.

Subconscious in critical thinking: A hidden resource for helping to do projects or achieving objectives.

Chapter 8
Fun with Comparison Studies

Comparison studies: Compare different products and services to determine the highest quality best value product. It is also called comparison shopping.

Selection criteria: Deciding on what features and/or options that are important to you when doing a comparison study such as price, quality/reliability and usefulness.

Weighing factor: The relative importance (ranking them) of each factor used in a comparison study.

Sweet spot: When the price of a product is low in comparison to the service life remaining.

Chapter 9
How to Make Wise Decisions

Left brain, right brain crossover: Using both the right and left parts of the brain to make sound, rational and logical decisions you can feel good about.

Domino effect: Aspects are interrelated in decision making. When important components are addressed, many of the lesser components are addressed as a natural side effect.

Thin slicing: The ability to focus on a small set of critical variables to make a quick decision rather than consciously considering every possible variable.

Razor sharp: Exceptional knowledge, reasoning, training, intuition, common sense, confidence and quickness.

Real time: At that moment.

Chapter 11
Discovering Your Multiple Intelligences

Convergent Thinking: Bringing together facts and data from various sources and then applying logic and knowledge to come up with a problem solution or to achieve an objective.

Divergent Thinking: Is thinking outwards instead of inward. It is the ability to develop original and unique ideas and then come up with a problem solution or achieve an objective.

Thought experiments: Imagined scenarios to understand the way things are.

Zone of potential: Areas in which a person can be successful at. Some individuals can flourish in several areas, others can be prosperous at one or two areas.

Chapter 12
Creating an Exciting Future for Yourself!

External questions: Questions asked to help define and complete projects, achieve objectives, solve problems and answer questions.

Internal questions: Questions asked to help improve your life.

Inflection point: An event that changes how you view the world, who you are, or your life in general.

Self-reflection: Taking an honest look at your strengths, weaknesses and what you want out of life.

Blue sky thinking: Sitting in a comfortable chair, getting a cup of warm tea, kicking back your feet and contemplating a deep subject.

The rocking chair test: A simple mental exercise that is done by imagining that you are in a rocking chair in the final years of your life. Ask yourself questions and use your personal history as a guide to help you decide on making any potential improvements to your future.

Cherry picking: To only do those things that most interest you.

Appendix B

Your Guide to Critical Thinking Concepts

The following is a list of the primary critical thinking concepts discussed in this book.

Chapter 1
Key Elements of Critical Thinking

There are many components to critical thinking. Some primary ones are:

- A Curious and Open Mind
- Thinking Though Issues
- Analyzing Issues from Multiple View Points
- Doing Needed Investigation
- Intuitive and Non-Intuitive Thinking

Chapter 2
Land Mines to Critical Thinking!

There are several land mines to critical thinking. The primary ones are:

- Egocentric Thinking
- Social Conditioning
- Biased Experience
- Arrogance and Intolerance
- Time and Patience
- Group Think—The Herd Mentality
- The Drone Mentality

Chapter 3
What are some Critical Questions?

Two critical questions that need to be asked when determining the validity of information are:

- Does this information make sense?
- What does my common sense; intuition, experience, and education tell me about this information?

Next, continually question:

- Information and Information sources
- Assumptions
- Interpretations and Implication
- Conclusions

Chapter 4
How to Solve Mysteries!

Below are some methods that can be used for doing tasks, solving problems and learning the mystery of how things work.

- The Scientific Method
- The 80/20 Rule

- Tinkering, the Art of Playing
- Locating the Root Cause of Problems
- Working Backwards
- Using History as a Guide

Chapter 5
How to Investigate any Subject

To effectively data mine use:

- Just in Time Learning

The following are common resources to doing investigation on any subject.

- The Internet
- Internet Bookstores
- Traditional Bookstores and Libraries
- Top Experts
- Local Experts
- Classes and Software

Chapter 6
How to Do Projects and Achieve Objectives

Here is a process for doing projects and achieving objectives.

Part I: Define your project or objective
Part II: Structure and then complete it

Step 1: Use your past knowledge
Step 2: Visualize your desired results

Step 3: Frame your project or objective

Step 4: Collect the facts and data

Step 5: Determine your available options

Step 6: Pick a solution and implement

Step 7: Modify or change if required

Step 8: Review your lessons learned

The Hidden Resource:

Your subconscious

Chapter 8
Fun with Comparison Studies

A comparison study focuses on primary elements of a product or service. The steps for doing a comparison study are straight forward. They are:

Step 1: Limit your search

Step 2: Investigate

Step 3: Reviewing the weighing factors

Step 4: Narrow your search

Step 5: Make your final selection

Chapter 9
How to Make Wise Decisions

There are several factors that affect your decisions. They are:

- Money
- Stress
- Time
- Facts, data and resources

The decision making process is:

1. Experience, book knowledge & common sense
2. Wisdom
3. Better decisions
4. More fun and a better existence

The seven steps for making effective decisions are:

Step 1—Gather the facts and data

Step 2—Make your assumptions

Step 3—Identify your options

Step 4—Use logic and common sense

Step 5—Incorporate your feelings

Step 6—Make your decision

Step 7—Modify or change your decision if needed

Here are some helpful decision making methods. They are:

- The Pareto Diagram (for comparison studies)
- The Ben Franklin Balance Sheet Close (for yes or no decisions)
- Thin Slicing (for quick decisions)

Chapter 10
How to Connect with Others

Here are some critical principles of good communication

Principle # 1: Our uniqueness affects how we communicate with others.

Principle #2: Being a student of people significantly increases our ability to communicate and connect with others.

Principle #3: Effective listening is an integral part of good communication.

Principle #4: Credibility coupled with sincerity, honesty and respect are the cornerstones of a fine reputation.

Principle # 5: It is important to carefully choose words and phrases when using remote forms of communication.

Principle #6: Helping others feel important will result in great service.

Principle #7: Conflicts are best managed by focusing on the issues rather than the individual.

Chapter 11
Discovering Your Multiple Intelligences

Here is a non-exhaustive list of human intelligences:

- Logical-Mathematical Intelligence
- Linguistic Intelligence
- Music Intelligence
- Bodily-Kinesthetic Intelligence
- Spatial-Intelligence
- Interpersonal Intelligence
- Intrapersonal Intelligence

Essential aspects of thinking are:

Convergent Thinking

Divergent Thinking

Chapter 12
Creating an Exciting Future for Yourself!

Here are some essential concepts for changing yourself:

- Using inflection points to improve your future
- Passion and Time Urgency
- Make a List and Check it Twice
- Visioning Your Own Future
- Finding Alternative Careers and Activities

Appendix C

Figures and Tables

The following is a list of the Figures and Tables in this book.

Chapter 1
Key Elements of Critical Thinking

Figure 1:   Intuitive and Non-Intuitive Thinking
Figure 2:   Stock Price Movement

Chapter 4
How to Solve Mysteries!

Figure 3:   The Scientific Method

Chapter 7
Critical Thinking Examples

Table 1:   The Australian Vacation Planning Form

Chapter 8
Fun with Comparison Studies

Figure 4:   Steps for Doing a Comparison Study

Figure 5:   A Normal Curve of Mustang Convertible Costs

Table 2:   Jack's Automobile Comparison Study Form

Chapter 9
How to Make Wise Decisions

Figure 6:   The Decision Making Process
Figure 7:   Steps for Effective Decision Making
Figure 8:   Jack's Logic Stream
Figure 9:   A Pareto Diagram of Appliance Electric Costs
Figure 10:   The Ben Franklin Balance Close Sheet

Table 3:   Appliance Costs and Power Usage

Chapter 11
Discovering Your Multiple Intelligences

Figure 11:   Convergent Thinking
Figure 12:   Divergent Thinking

Appendix D
Vacation Planning Forms

Table 1:   The Australian Vacation Planning Form
Table 4:   Your Vacation Planning Form

Appendix E
Comparison Study Forms

Table 2:   Jack's Automobile Comparison Study Form
Table 5:   Your Automobile Comparison Study Form
Table 6:   Your Blank Comparison Study Form

Appendix D

Vacation Planning Forms

To predict the expected costs of a vacation noted in Chapter 6 (How to do Projects and Achieve Objectives) an example was provided. It is reproduced below.

A blank form is provided to assist you on planning your next vacation.

Note: This form can be recreated in Microsoft® Excel® or any other spreadsheet program if you would rather customize your own form.

Activity	Cost per day (each person)	Number of days	Number of days	Number of excursions	Average cost per excursion	Total expected cost
Travel Expenses						
• Airfare to: Sydney A.						$ 1,330
• Car Rental						$ -
Gas						$ -
Hotel Expenses (Inc Tax)	$ 60	7				$ 420
Food	$ 65	7				$ 455
Excursions				4	$ 70	$ 280
Gifts, souvenirs, Etc						$ 120
Miscellaneous Expenses						$ 200
Expected costs						$ 2,805

The Australia Vacation Planning Form
(Table 1 Reproduced)

Activity	Cost per day (each person)	Number of days	Number of days	Number of excursions	Average cost per excursion	Total expected cost
Travel Expenses						
◆ Airfare to:						
◆ Car Rental						
Gas						
Hotel Expenses (Inc Tax)						
Food						
Excursions						
Gifts, trinkets, Etc						
Miscellaneous Expenses						
Expected costs						$

Your Vacation Planning Form
Table 4

Appendix E

Comparison Study Forms

To do a comparison study on automobiles Chapter 8 (Fun with Comparison Studies) provided an example. It is reproduced below.

Two more forms have been provided for your use. First, a blank form is provided to assist on when purchasing your next vehicle.

Second, a blank generic comparison study form is provided for your use on items such as appliances, cell phones, computers, credit cards or any other product you would like to do a comparison study on.

Note: These forms can be recreated in Microsoft® Excel® or any other spreadsheet program if you would rather customize your own forms.

No.	Make & Model	Price Range	Used Car (2-4 yrs)	Quality & Reliability	Utility (Sporty)	Looks	Approx. Gas mileage (Miles per Gallon - MPG)	Depreciation	Handling	Power	Company
1	Ford Mustang Convertible	$18-24K	Y	VG	E	E	20-26	F	G	G	G
2	Honda Accord	$18-22K	Y	E	F	G	30-40	F	G	G	E
3	Acura TSX	$24-29K	Y	E	G	E	22-30	F	G	G	E
4	Toyota Corolla	$17-21K	Y	E	F	P	30-38	F	G	G	E
	Jack's Requirements	$18-24K	Y	VG	G	G	20-24	F	G	G	G

Y =Yes
N= No

P = Poor
F = Fair
G = Good
VG = Very Good
E = Excellent

Jack's Automobile Comparison Study Form
(Table 2 Reproduced)

No.	Make & Model	Price Range	Used Car (2-4 yrs)	Quality & Reliability	Utility (Sporty)	Looks and personality	Approx. Gas mileage (Miles per Gallon -MPG)	Depreciation	Handling	Power	Company
1											
2											
3											
4											
	Your Requirements										

Y = Yes
N= No

P = Poor
F = Fair
G = Good
VG = Very Good
E = Excellent

Your Automobile Comparison Study Form
Table 5

No.	Product									
1										
2										
3										
4										
	Your Requirements									

Y = Yes
N = No

P = Poor
F = Fair
G = Good
VG = Very Good
E = Excellent

Your Blank Comparison Study Form
Table 6

Appendix F

Illustrations

The following are a list of cartoons and pictures in this book.

Introduction

- Critical Thinking!

Chapter 1
Key Elements of Critical Thinking

- Flowing Down the Stream of Logic
- Mt Everest
- Crawling out of One's Box

Chapter 2
Land Mines to Critical Thinking!

- Land Mines to Critical Thinking
- David Crocket's Hat
- Sidestepping the Land Mines

Chapter 4
How to Solve Mysteries!

- Solving the Mystery
- Picking your Dragons Carefully
- The Hole in the Wall Project
- The Broken Windows theory

Chapter 5
How to Investigate any Subject

- Investigating!

Chapter 7
Critical Thinking Examples

- The Finished Home Patio

Chapter 8
Fun with Comparison Studies

- Choosing the Right Car!

Chapter 9
How to Make Wise Decisions

- The Left Brain, Right Brain Crossover
- Home Appliances
- The Domino Effect

Chapter 10
How to Connect with Others

- Connections book

Chapter 11
Discovering Your Multiple Intelligences

- Logical-Mathematical Intelligence
- Linguistic Intelligence
- Music Intelligence
- Bodily-Kinesthetic Intelligence
- Spatial-Intelligence
- Interpersonal Intelligence
- Intrapersonal Intelligence
- Moon Landing

Chapter 12
Creating an Exciting Future for Yourself!

- Which Future?

About the Author

Chuck Clayton's primary education and professional experience is in mechanical engineering and business problem solving. He has over thirty years experience in these areas. Chuck has a BSME from Michigan Tech University, and an MBA from Pepperdine University. Chuck is also an Advanced Communicator Silver Toastmaster.

Chuck Clayton has an insatiable curiosity of the world and how things work. This has guided him to research and learn efficient ways of making decisions, solving problems and organizing the thinking process to improve quality, be more productive and free up time. He is the author of *Connections—For Communication that Works*. It is an excellent companion for *The Re-Discovery of Common Sense*.

Chuck lives in Tucson Arizona. He enjoys active sports, studies the history and lessons of the Apollo space program, dances Argentine Tango, and travels when possible.

For more information please see:

www.chuckclayton.com

~Notes~

~Notes~

~Notes~

~Notes~

~Notes~

~Notes~

978-0-595-43708-5
0-595-43708-7

Printed in the United States
212722BV00001B/7/A